Cambridge E

Elements in Ancient E
edited by
Gianluca Miniaci
University of Pisa
Juan Carlos Moreno García
CNRS, Paris
Anna Stevens
University of Cambridge and Monash University

T0277522

ETHNIC IDENTITIES IN THE LAND OF THE PHARAOHS

Past and Present Approaches in Egyptology

Uroš Matić
Austrian Archaeological Institute

CAMBRIDGE
UNIVERSITY PRESS

CAMBRIDGE
UNIVERSITY PRESS

University Printing House, Cambridge CB2 8BS, United Kingdom

One Liberty Plaza, 20th Floor, New York, NY 10006, USA

477 Williamstown Road, Port Melbourne, VIC 3207, Australia

314–321, 3rd Floor, Plot 3, Splendor Forum, Jasola District Centre,
New Delhi – 110025, India

79 Anson Road, #06–04/06, Singapore 079906

Cambridge University Press is part of the University of Cambridge.

It furthers the University's mission by disseminating knowledge in the pursuit of
education, learning, and research at the highest international levels of excellence.

www.cambridge.org
Information on this title: www.cambridge.org/9781108794466
DOI: 10.1017/9781108885577

First published 2020

A catalogue record for this publication is available from the British Library.

ISBN 978-1-108-79446-6 Paperback
ISSN 2516-4813 (online)
ISSN 2516-4805 (print)

Ethnic Identities in the Land of the Pharaohs

Past and Present Approaches in Egyptology

Elements in Ancient Egypt in Context

DOI: 10.1017/9781108885577
First published online: November 2020

Uroš Matić
Austrian Archaeological Institute
Author for correspondence: Uroš Matić, uros.matic@oeai.at

Abstract: *Ethnic Identities in the Land of the Pharaohs* deals with the ancient Egyptian concept of collective identity, various groups which inhabited the Egyptian Nile Valley and different approaches to ethnic identity in the last two hundred years of Egyptology. The aim is to present the dynamic processes of ethnogenesis of the inhabitants of the land of the pharaohs, and to place various approaches to ethnic identity in their broader scholarly and historical context. The dominant approach to ethnic identity in ancient Egypt is still based on the culture-historical method. This and other theoretically better-framed approaches (e.g. instrumentalist approach, habitus, postcolonial approach, ethnogenesis, intersectionality) are discussed using numerous case studies from the third millennium to the first century BC. Finally, this Element deals with the recent impact of the third science revolution on archaeological research on ethnic identity in ancient Egypt.

Keywords: ancient Egypt, ethnicity, culture-historical archaeology, habitus, scientific racism

ISBNs: 9781108794466 (PB), 9781108885577 (OC)
ISSNs: 2516–4813 (online), 2516–4805 (print)

Contents

'Today these are troubled waters which most people who write about ancient Egypt from within the mainstream of scholarship avoid.'

B. J. Kemp (2018: 47)

1 Introduction

This Element introduces various readers to ancient Egyptian collective identity and Egyptological research on ethnicity. The chronological boundaries will not play a significant role here; still, each case discussed in the text will be chronologically and geographically framed. Most of the provided examples are from the third and second millennium BC in Egypt and Nubia, which is the period of my scholarly interest. However, as this Element should serve to give readers an overview of works on ethnic identity and ethnicity in Egyptology, examples from first millennium BC are also provided.

It is not possible to summarise ancient Egyptian history in great detail in a single passage without using Egyptology specific terms such as dynasties, kingdoms, or intermediate periods. Still, several phases of Egyptian history are referred to throughout this Element and it is therefore necessary to summarise them. The formation of the ancient Egyptian state started around 3200 BC in the Naqada region in Upper Egypt. By around 3000 BC, this proto-state expanded to include Lower Egypt and establish domination over southern Levant. It also had contact and conflict with the population in Lower Nubia. Around 2700 BC, began a period of monumental funerary constructions (pyramids), building of monumental temples, and expeditions to foreign lands such as Byblos in Lebanon, Nubia (Sudan), and Punt at the Horn of Africa. Around 2200 BC, the state lost its control of the provinces where local rulers slowly but surely took over. The domain of the successor state was limited to Lower Egypt. In Upper Egypt, local rulers of Thebes managed to defeat their rivals and form their own kingdom. They eventually defeated the state in Lower Egypt and united the land around 2055 BC. Since the unification, more investment is seen in monumental architecture again. Military fortresses were built in Lower Nubia to support the expeditions and diminish the threat from even further south (Kerma in Upper Nubia). Eastern Delta, a corridor to Egypt with mixed population since prehistory, became the entry point for population from the Levant. There is evidence for close ties with Byblos. Around 1800 BC, the state again lost its power in the provinces and its fortresses in Lower Nubia. Rulers of foreign origin known as the Hyksos took over the control of Eastern Delta and later on of the entire Lower Egypt. The kingdom of Kush, centred in Kerma, took control of Egyptian military fortresses in Lower Nubia. The kings centred in Thebes, now had to fight the Hyksos state in the north and the kingdom of Kush in the south. They eventually defeated their rivals and united the land around 1550 BC. This is when a period of expansion began. Egypt took control of both Levant and

Nubia. Egyptians settled in Nubia and built military fortresses in the Levant. Egypt had close contacts with Aegean polities from fifteenth to fourteenth century BC, but also conflict with state Mitanni and eventually with the Hittite state in which it lost control of the northern Levant. Conflicts with the Libyans in the west and the incursion of various groups of Sea People marauders brought new challenges to the pharaohs. Around 1100 BC, Egypt lost control of its domains in both Levant and Nubia and faced internal fractured rule as it also lost its control of Thebes where priests of Amun became powerful. The state in this period was divided between the kings of Egypt ruling in Lower Egypt and the priests and god Amun ruling in Middle and Upper Egypt. A rival state was slowly but surely also forming in Nubia, now under control of the locals. Around 950 BC, Egypt was united again for a century or so, and after that again fell into a fragmentary state, with several parallel dynasties and rulers of Libyan origin controlling different parts of the country. Around 750 BC, the Nubian rulers took this opportunity and defeated different dynasties in Egypt, establishing a double kingdom. They were in war with Assyria, which was their downfall around 670 BC. Egypt was left to a local dynasty which ruled the country until around 530 BC when the Achamenide Persian empire expanded to Egypt. In 332 BC, Alexander the Great defeated Persian-controlled Egypt and a Ptolemaic state was formed in 305 BC and ruled by a dynasty of Macedonian origin. This dynasty was eventually a client state of Rome and was defeat in 31 BC by Octavian August who made Egypt into a Roman province in 30 BC. From fourth to sixth century AD, Christian Roman Egypt was a diocese, regional governance district in the late Roman empire. Around 650 AD, it was conquered by the Arabs.

During this more than 3,000-year-long history, both how ancient Egyptians viewed themselves and others and which foreigners lived among them was changing. Therefore, three main questions will be addressed in this Element:

a) How did ancient Egyptians understand their own collective identity in comparison to their neighbours and other foreigners, and can this be translated into a modern concept such as ethnic identity? Answering this question is important because we need to balance ancient concepts and our translations of these concepts into our own vocabulary and theoretical discourses.

b) How did early scholars in the nineteenth and early twentieth century approach ancient Egyptians and their neighbours and are there remnants of their ideas in contemporary Egyptology? The reason this question has to be addressed is that more often than not certain ideas belonging to a disciplinary past emerge in a new form in contemporary scholarship (Matić, 2018a).

c) How do modern scholars approach various groups inhabiting the Egyptian Nile Valley? Are contemporary discussions on ethnic identity useful in approaching ancient Egypt? We need to critically reflect on the concepts we use in order to better understand how they form our interpretations and what we can do to balance the premodern–modern dichotomy.

1.1 The Categories of Evidence

Egyptology is a discipline dealing with the history, society, language, and culture of ancient Egypt. Although often criticised because of its narrow philological focus on ancient Egyptian texts and language, there have been considerable developments in the last few decades which also turn attention to more up-to-date understanding of archaeology and art history (Kemp, 2018; Verbovsek, Backes & Jones, 2011; Wendrich, 2010). Depending on the period of ancient Egyptian history they focus on, Egyptologists are in a unique position in comparison to other scholars dealing with ancient cultures because of the rich visual, textual, and archaeological evidence at hand. The categories of evidence important for studying ethnic identity in ancient Egypt are:

1 Visual Sources
Subjugating the enemy is a motif known in ancient Egyptian iconography since around 3500 BC (Köhler, 2002: 511) and detailed depictions of enemies from around 3200 to 3000 BC predate the first texts mentioning various groups of enemies (Bestock, 2018). These testify to already developed ideas on 'us' and 'them'. For example, already on the so-called Libyan palette from this period, a throwstick hieroglyph is used in association with seven towns depicted being destroyed. This sign is later used to designate *Ṯmḥ.w* or *Ṯḥn.w* Libyan groups, as Egyptians called some of their neighbours in the west (de Wit, 2015: 650). By the time the hieroglyphic script appears in its fully developed form, we can also recognise specific types of enemies in iconography. Traditional enemies and neighbours of Egypt in the south-Nubians, the north-Syro-Palestianians and the west-Libyans are a recurrent motif in ancient Egyptian art over several millennia (Figure 2; Roth, 2015). We find them as bound captives or as enemies on the battlefield, but also as trade partners and inhabitants of Egypt of different status and occupations (e.g. slaves, soldiers, musicians, dancers). The contexts in which their representations are found in different periods of ancient Egyptian history range from small objects such as palettes, throne chairs, cosmetic vessels, wooden boxes, walking sticks, weapons, chariots, and sandals to paintings and reliefs on the walls of private and royal tombs and state temples (Anthony, 2016; Hallmann, 2006; Roth, 2015; Saretta, 2016). The common denominator behind these contexts is their elite background. Such representations provide us with a specific view of a small percentage of the society with its own agenda and politics. The

advantages of visual representations of foreigners are not only that they provide us with information on ancient Egyptian neighbours, but also that they provide us with a specifically elite ancient Egyptian view of these peoples and the criteria of difference. The disadvantage of visual representations is that they provide us neither with the perspective of ancient Egyptian non-elites, which in some contexts could have been different, nor with the perspective of those depicted. These ideologically framed and culturally relative depictions of foreigners were sometimes approached as accurate representations of reality (for details see Section 2). However, several cases demonstrate that this was actually not entirely the case (for details see Section 3).

2 Written Sources

The first written sources on foreigners in ancient Egypt appear very early, *c.*3200–3000 BC, in the form of signs indicating foreign toponyms and ethnonyms, as we have seen in the case of the Libyan palette. Already on the ivory label of King Den from Abydos from the beginning of third millennium BC, an easterner is depicted and his origin from the East is indicated in the accompanying text (Köhler, 2002: 504–5). Later on, starting from about mid third millennium BC (Gundacker, 2017; Saretta, 2016), foreigners are mentioned regularly in different texts ranging from private elite autobiographies, royal texts on stelae, temple walls, and administrative documents to literary texts in which foreigners can also be some of the key figures (Di Biase-Dyson, 2013; Loprieno, 1988). The advantage of the written sources is that they provide us with personal names and places of origin of foreigners, but also descriptions of their appearance and customs (Hinson, 2014). The disadvantage of written sources is that the image of foreigners we obtain from them was in fact probably not the image foreigners had of themselves. The way they are described, named and grouped by the ancient Egyptians was ordered by many factors and does not directly reflect the reality of foreign identities. Whenever we read an ancient Egyptian text describing foreigners we should ask ourselves who wrote it, when, for which audience, and why?

3 Foreign Material Culture in Ancient Egypt and Ancient Egyptian Material Culture in Foreign Contexts

The most often used evidence for exchange and trade with the neighbouring countries and regions, but also for tracing foreign presence in Egypt is the material culture of foreign origin. This category among other things includes foreign pottery, jewelry, and weaponry. Considerable amounts of foreign material culture made out of organic materials is rarely preserved, but its presence in Egypt is indicated by written and visual sources. The main disadvantage of foreign material culture in Egypt or Egyptian material culture in foreign contexts is that it is often extremely difficult to differentiate between an object imported through exchange and trade on one side, and an object imported by a travelling or a resident foreigner on the other. Although modern application of techniques from physical, chemical, biological, and earth sciences and engineering, to address archaeological questions and problems, can sometimes provide us with the origin of the raw material from which these objects were made, 'foreign' objects could have also been made in local materials by foreigners or imitated in local or imported materials by Egyptians. The fact that not only objects can travel, but also artisans and raw materials, significantly complicates the assumptions on origins no matter the analyses involved (Feldman, 2006). The same is valid for Egyptian material culture outside of Egypt, which can equally be imported through exchange and trade or through actual presence of an Egyptian. The underlying problem is that foreign material culture in Egypt and Egyptian material culture in foreign contexts is more often than not interpreted as evidence for foreign or Egyptian presence and as such connected to the question of ethnic identity. This is especially the case when foreign material culture in Egypt is found in a burial in Egypt or when Egyptian material culture is found in a burial outside of Egypt. If the burial also indicates Egyptian or foreign burial customs, the case is taken as prime example of a foreigner in Egypt or an Egyptian in a foreign land. The associated problems behind such assumptions are extensively discussed in Section 2.

4 Skeletal Remains
Skeletal remains have been used to identify ancient Egyptians and foreigners since the establishment of Egyptology as a discipline in the nineteenth century. Although methods used to identify them changed from initial craniometrical measures and racial assumptions (Section 2), to modern methods such as analyses of ancient DNA and isotope analyses (Section 4), the underlying assumption is more often than not that ethnic identity is something written in the body. The advantage of skeletal remains is that DNA and isotope analyses can, among other things, provide us with clues on the origin of a person, where they were born, spent their life, and eventually died. However, these information should not be confused with ethnic identity, which is a social construct related to a person's feeling of belonging to a certain group, on one side, and the way others perceive the identity of this person, on the other (Section 3).

1.2 Terms

Often, explicit theoretical and methodological statements in Egyptology are lacking in research on social phenomena, such as ethnic identity and ethnicity. Like in other archaeologies, few people actually explicitly define what they mean by ethnic group or ethnicity (Jones, 1997: 56). The standard reference works in Egyptology, such as *Lexikon der Ägyptologie* or *The Oxford Encyclopedia of Ancient Egypt*, do not contain entries on ethnicity (Helck, 1977a; Helck, 1977b; Gordon, 2001). Some, like *The British Museum Dictionary of Ancient Egypt*, even have an entry on race (Shaw & Nicholson, 1995: 239; see Section 2). Although slowly but surely appearing in works of Egyptologists (e.g. Goudriaan, 1988; Köhler, 2002) and extensively discussed by S. T. Smith (2003b), the first entry on ethnicity in a standard reference work of encyclopedic format appeared relatively late in *UCLA Encyclopedia of Egyptology* (Riggs & Baines, 2012). Thus, discussions on ethnicity outside of Egyptology have gradually entered the discipline quite recently and are still largely unknown even to most Egyptologists. This is why it is important to start with a short list and definitions of terms frequently encountered in this Element:

1.   Ancient Egypt designates a civilisation of ancient northern Africa primarily concentrated in the Nile Valley from the Nile Delta in the north to the First Cataract (shallow length where the water is broken by many small boulders) on the Nile in the south (Figure 1). Ancient Egyptians called their land *Kmt* 'black land' referring to fertile soil of the Nile Valley; *T3-mry* 'beloved land' indicating an emotional relationship to their land; *T3-wy* 'two lands', a dual referring to both Lower Egypt (*T3-mḥ.w* or *T3-bity*), from Nile Delta to Memphis (one of the ancient capitals), and Upper Egypt (*T3-šmᶜ.w*), from Memphis to Elephantine on the First Cataract (Kilani, 2015: 75).

The ancient Egyptian state, which initially developed in the region of Naqada in Upper Egypt around 3200 BC, first expended its territory to include the rest of Upper Egypt and then Lower Egypt. In the course of its history, this state managed to establish and lose its control of different own and neighbouring regions such as Lower Nubia (from First to Second Cataract on the Nile) and Upper Nubia (from Second to Sixth Cataract on the Nile) in the south and the Levant in the north (Morris, 2018). Therefore, when talking about ancient Egypt and ancient Egyptians we have to bear in mind that these terms do not refer to a static society resistant to demographic, social, and cultural change (Schneider, 2003). Strictly speaking there is no such thing as 'ancient Egypt' and 'ancient Egyptians'. The land we refer to as ancient Egypt, although having its core in the Nile Valley from the Delta to the First Cataract, either expanded or lost parts of its territories only to regain control of them again. The people we refer to with the term ancient Egyptians were men, women, and children of different class backgrounds living in different towns and regions of the land. Some of them had foreign origins; others were married to foreigners or to people of foreign origin. Some never left their villages, towns, or regions; others travelled far away and

Figure 1 Map of Egypt and Sudan with sites frequently referred to in the
Element (graphic by A. Hassler, ÖAI/ÖAW).

frequently. Some spoke only ancient Egyptian language; others spoke other languages too. A small percentage of the population was fully literate; a large percentage was of limited literacy or no literacy at all. Some of them lived in land ruled by a ruler of local origin and some in a land ruled by a ruler of foreign origin. This diversity is important to stress from the very beginning and it will be extensively discussed throughout the Element.

2.   Race designates biological variations inscribed with explanatory value. Scientific racism implies that physical attributes (mostly external, such as, e.g. skin and hair colour) or morphological features of the skeleton (more often than not the cranium) correspond to inner mental capacities (Siapkas, 2014: 68). According to modern physical anthropology major features of human biological diversity are polymorphic (variation within a group being quantitatively predominant), clinal (i.e. structured as gradients), and culturally mediated. Folk taxonomies of races are culture specific, as they develop from unique historical and demographic factors. Therefore, agglomeration of physically diverse peoples into 'races' is culturally determined (Williams, Belcher & Armelagos, 2005: 340–2). There is no biological validity for the racial construct (Zakrzewski, Shortland & Rowland, 2016: 219–20). For example, M. Hefny, an Egyptian immigrant to the USA, considered himself to be black. According to the rules of USA government on race and ethnicity from 1997, all people originating in Europe, the Middle East, and North Africa are classified as white. Hefny filed a lawsuit to change his official classification from white to black (Saini, 2019: 4). Ancient Egyptians did not have the concept of race, as their attitudes towards peoples were based on cultural status and not colour (Foster, 1974: 187). Therefore, the concept of race, although paramount for Egyptology of the nineteenth and early twentieth century, has no scientific credibility in modern scholarship. Section 2 of this Element deals with the problem of race and scientific racism in Egyptology because, although not based in modern anthropology, these concept continue to exist in one form or another even in some recent works.

3.   Archaeological culture was best defined by Australian born archaeologist V. G. Childe (1892–1957) who argued that: 'We find certain types of remains pots, implements, ornaments, burial rites and house forms constantly recurring together. Such a complex of associated traits we shall call a "cultural group" or just a "culture". We assume that such a complex is the material expression of what today we would call "a people".' (Childe, 1929: v–vi)

The concept of archaeological culture was marked by a modernist understanding of a nation state – a unity of territory, material culture, language, and ethnic affiliation (Sherratt, 2005: 27; Thomas, 2004: 112). G. Kossina (1858–1931), German linguist and archaeologist, developed an ethnic paradigm which he called 'settlement archaeology' with the basic premise that artefact types could be used to identify cultures and that clearly distinguishable cultural provinces reflect the settlement areas of past tribes or ethnic groups (Jones, 1997: 2). This approach is quintessential for the so-called culture-historical or traditional archaeology.

Section 2 of this Element deals with the use of the premises of culture-historical archaeology on material culture and ethnic identity in Egyptology. Although a theoretical position with flaws which have been recognised since 1960s, culture-historical archaeology is still the dominant way of thinking in archaeology, including archaeology of Egypt. This is why it is necessary to point again to its pitfalls and demonstrate them with several examples.

4. Ethnicity is a concept with a complex history (Jones, 1997; McInerney, 2014: 2). The word comes from the ancient Greek word *ethnos* which primarily denoted a group of beings, humans or animals, which share certain characteristics and form a group. Its use to designate different groups of foreigners is more related to the fifth century BC and the writings of Herodotus (Isaac, 2004: 112; Sherratt, 2005: 31; Siapkas, 2014: 67). The concept of ethnicity can include many aspects and their combination results in a group identifying itself as a people (McInerney, 2014: 2). M. Weber (1864–1920), German sociologist, has already argued for many notions of ethnicity found in later scholarship, such as those that ethnic groups are social constructs, based on a subjective belief in a shared community (Jenkins, 2008: 10).

Ethnic labels are not fixed because the identities and the relations to which they are applied are in a constant flux of inclusion and exclusion (McInerney, 2014: 3). According to M. Fischer, ethnicity is 'reinvented and reinterpreted with each generation by each individual. . . . Ethnicity is not something that is simply passed on from generation to generation, taught and learned; it is something dynamic, often unsuccessfully repressed or avoided' (Fischer, 1986: 195). It is not so much a 'deep-seated force surviving from the historical past', but a process (Sollors, 1989: xiv–xv). The task of archaeologists who attempt to research ethnic identity is to identify those who choose to act or look the same, and then to explore the contexts in which they do so and whether these changed over time (Lucy, 2005: 108).

The key reference in archaeological studies of ethnicity in the last two decades has been the monograph *Archaeology of Ethnicity* by S. Jones (1997). According to Jones, ethnic identity is 'that aspect of a person's self-conceptualisation which results from identification with a broader group in opposition to others on the basis of perceived cultural differentiation and/or common descent' (Jones, 1997: 13). She understands ethnic identification as involving objectification of cultural practices (unconscious behaviour) in the recognition and signification of difference in opposition to others (Jones, 1997: 128). According to Jones 'ethnicity is a product of the intersection of similarities and differences in people's habitus and the conditions characterising any given historical situation' (Jones, 1997: 126). For example, she argues that domestic architecture such as bath houses and villas in Roman Britain were an important part of the habitus, and these may have been involved in recognition and signification of a broad Roman identity (Jones, 1997: 134). Section 3 deals with various contemporary Egyptological approaches to ethnic identity and ethnicity in ancient Egypt. Using several examples, this section will discuss how ethnic identities in ancient Egypt have to be approached bearing in mind their diverse social and historical contexts.

5.   Habitus is a term primarily associated in sociology with P. Bourdieu (1930–2002) and his theory of practice. According to Bourdieu it is composed of 'systems of durable, transposable dispositions, structured structures predisposed to function as structuring structures, that is, as principles which generate and organize practices and representations that can be objectively adapted to their outcomes without presupposing a conscious aiming at ends or an express mastery of the operations necessary in order to attain them' (Bourdieu, 1990: 53).

   According to R. Jenkins, habitus is 'the embodied and unreflexive everyday practical mastery of culture: unsystematic, the empire of habit, neither conscious nor unconscious' (Jenkins, 2008: 79). Crucial for the concept of habitus is that it involves unconscious dispositions people share towards certain perceptions and practices such as daily tasks, labour skills, cooking, cleaning, dressing, etc. Within this context, ethnic identity is understood as the result of the intersection of one's habitual dispositions and the social conditions in existence within a particular historical context (Curta, 2014: 2508). The reconceptualisation of Bourdieu's habitus is related to the work of G. C. Bentley who argued that 'sensations of ethnic affinity are founded on common life experiences that generate similar habitual dispositions' (Bentley, 1987: 32). The concept of habitus has seen increased attention by scholars studying ethnic identity in ancient Egypt and will be discussed on several examples in Section 3.

1.3 Being Egyptian and Being Foreign: Over 3000 Years of Ethnogenesis

'Egyptian' could be anyone who inhabited the urban zones of the Nile Valley (Assmann, 1996: 97; Espinel, 2006: 452; Moers, 2001: 177), spoke Egyptian language, worshipped Egyptian gods, and was loyal to the Egyptian state, no matter if he or she was born in Egypt or not.

Where language is concerned, non-Egyptians were considered by Egyptians to babble and the same word was used for the braying of a donkey (Johnson, 1999: 212). Similarly, the ancient Greek word *barbaros*, a reduplicative onomatopoeia, originally described the incomprehensible speech of any foreign language, later to acquire the meaning of a non-Greek (Heath, 2005: 199). Egyptian language was seen as one of the main criteria of Egyptianess since at least the beginning of second millennium BC and even the Greek historian Herodotus writes that Egyptians are those who live downriver from Elephantine and drink the Nile water (II 18, 3) and foreigners are those who do not speak their language (II 158, 5) (Kammerzell, 1993: 183).

Those who inhabited non-urban zones outside of the Nile Valley (e.g. marshlands, [Hawkins, 2012] and the desert) or foreign lands, did not speak Egyptian, did not worship Egyptian gods, and potentially threatened the Egyptian state were considered to be foreign. Of course, in different periods and contexts these factors come in different constellations. Foreign lands were considered undesirable to die in by Egyptians because of the danger of not being properly buried. Already in the biography of Sabni, son of Menkhu I, from around 2280 BC, it is written that after he died in Lower Nubia his body was returned to Egypt and buried by his son (Gundacker, 2017: 347). This concern over burial in Egypt is also evident in the *Story of Sinuhe* from early second millennium BC, when Sinuhe, an Egyptian official, who after fleeing from Egypt to the Levant desires to go back to Egypt and asks what is more important than being buried in Egypt (Allen, 2015: 111). In the *Story of Wemanun* from eleventh century BC, when Wenamun found himself in Byblos (modern Lebanon), he refused to see the gravesite of Egyptian emissaries who died abroad (Di Biase-Dyson, 2013: 336). Being buried back in Egypt was related to being close to the place of one's life on earth even in death.

According to J. Assmann and G. Moers, the ancient Egyptians did not have the concepts of ethnic or national belonging and expressed their identity in relation to family, village, or town and in connection to kinship, familiarity, and trust (Assmann, 1996: 97; Moers, 2016). Localism as a crucial aspect of Egyptian identity and being buried in one's own city meant that the family and friends of the deceased could assure one's further existence through offerings (Espinel, 2006: 452). This localism probably influenced regional differences. There is evidence that the inhabitants of the Nile Valley considered the population of the Delta to be as different from the population of Upper Egypt as an Egyptian is different from someone from the Levant. In the *Story of Sinuhe*, he describes himself after fleeing to the Levant from Egypt 'like a Deltan seeing himself in Elephantine, like a man of the marshland in Bowland (Nubia)' (Allen, 2015: 130). Hundreds of years later, similar binary opposition is attested in the Papyrus Anastasi I (40, 3–4) from early thirteenth century BC, where 'the speech of a Delta man with a man from Elephantine' is attested (Haring, 2005: 162). These texts testify to ancient Egyptian awareness of differences between people of their own land being comparable to the differences between them and foreigners.

There are also texts which mention criteria of difference recognised by ancient Egyptians between themselves and others. Papyrus Bulaq 17 from fifteenth century BC, invokes the creator god Atum and describes him in the following way: 'Atum who has made the population, who has distinguished their characters, who has made them live, who has distinguished their colours, one from the other' (Wilson, 1969: 365–6). The Great Hymn to Aten from fourteenth century BC found in the tomb of the courier and later king Ay is particularly important as it provides us with a parallel for the earlier Papyrus Bulaq 17 when the division of mankind is concerned:

> You created the world in your fashion, you alone; this world of men, of herds, and of wild beasts, of all that is on the earth and walks on legs, of all that is in the air and flies with wings outstretched. Of all the foreign lands, from Syria to Nubia and the land of Egypt. You set every man in his place. You supplied their necessities. Everyone has his food, and his time of life is reckoned. Their tongues (*ns.w*) are separate in speech (*md.t*) and their natures (*kd=sn*) as well; Their skins (*jnm=sn*) are distinguished, as you distinguished the foreign peoples. (Lichtheim, 1976: 98)

It seems that what distinguishes people are the languages they speak, the forms/characters they have and the colour of their skin. This choice of characteristics to distinguish people is very interesting. S. T. Smith interprets it as 'remarkably modern textual and visual construction of ethnicity, representing ethnic groups as essentialized, distinctive traditions, bounded in space and time' (Smith, 2014: 195). That Aten distinguished people according to these features did not stop Heqanefer, who had Nubian origin, from depicting himself as an Egyptian (*kd*-form) having different skin colour (*jnm*) and speaking different language (*ns.w md.t*) than Aten (or the Egyptians) would attribute to Nubians (see Section 3 for detailed discussion). A parallel is found in the *Story of Sinuhe* when Sinuhe the Egyptian is described returning to Egypt by one of the king's children as an 'Asiatic that the Asiatics have created' (Allen, 2015: 142). Asiatic is a term Egyptologists conventionally use as translation of ancient Egyptian word *ᶜ3 m.w* referring to the inhabitants of Syria-Palestine.

Whereas some texts indicate essentialised view of Egyptians and foreigners regarding their appearance and language, other texts and representations indicate that appearance and language were subject to change, leading to a change of both self-identification and perception by others. Ancient

Egyptian art used skin colour to differentiate between Egyptians (reddish), Nubians (brown and black), Syro-Palestinians (yellowish), and Libyans (whitish-yellowish), which could easily lead one to false conclusion that skin colour was considered to be essential for one's identity. Still, Aegeans ('Minoans') and Puntites are also depicted with reddish skin colour like Egyptians (Anthony, 2016) in fifteenth century BC Egyptian art, indicating that they share something with Egyptians other foreigners do not. There is no evidence that Egypt was in conflict with the Aegean polities and the land of Punt at this time; rather the contrary, these lands are trading partners and are in ancient Egyptian cultural geography located at the very ends of the known world. Even Egyptian gods dwell there, as we know of Horus from Crete and Amun from Punt. It is our task to pay attention to the context of both essentialised and volatile understanding of Egyptianness and otherness. Pronounced differences between Egyptians and some foreigners or similiarities with others could also reflect cosmology and politics (Kilani, 2015). In fact, ancient Egyptians used the word *rmṯ* 'human' to designate both themselves and foreigners, and 'humanity' was something both Egyptians and foreigners could lose (Chantrain, 2019; Moers, 2005).

From around 2700 to 1650 BC, most of the ethnonyms we encounter in textual sources are rather generic and are used by Egyptians themselves as umbrella terms for various groups (Asiatics or Syro-Palestinians, Nubians, Libyans, and inhabitants of the Eastern Desert). From around 1600 BC and later, there is increased contact with more distant foreign lands and new ethnonyms appear in Egyptian sources, some old ones changed meanings and new foreign groups are attested in Egypt (e.g. Aegeans, various groups we label as Sea Peoples, Hittites). Some of them, like Sea People Shardana men, fought both against Egyptians and on their side since thirteenth to twelfth century BC, and eventually stayed in Egypt where they married Egyptian women and were depicted as Egyptian men worshiping Egyptian gods, the epithet Shardana being the only indication of their foreign origin (Emanuel, 2013). One still finds those with Asiatic or Nubian descent, sometimes keeping to their foreign origin, sometimes keeping only the name of their ancestors. For those people who seem to us to be foreign only because of their name or the name of some of their ancestors, we should be very careful in dismissing the possibility that they were seen as less Egyptian than foreign by their contemporaries. If and in which contexts their Egyptianness could be questioned is, according to the best of my knowledge, not known yet. Foreign ancestry can be invisible in documents if the name is Egyptian and, as also suggested, could be omitted for reasons of decorum, status, or profession (Mourad, 2017: 384). Sometimes although the names were foreign, the titles of these 'foreigners' were Egyptian, as were their burials and the rest of their dress (e.g in the tomb of three foreign wives of Thutmose III from fifteenth century BC; Lilyquist, 2003). They do not seem to be considered less Egyptian than other Egyptians and maybe this was so because of their status.

This trend continues in the first two centuries of first millennium BC, when local kings of Libyan descent and those kings coming from Kush ruled the country. In those cases where we can recognise people of foreign origin, this is again because of their names (Johnson, 1999: 212) or, in some cases, certain cultural elements such as dress. G. Vittmann stresses that Libyan royal names, such as Osorkon, Shoshenk, and Psammtich are attested even until the Ptolemaic period, from fourth to first century BC (Vittmann, 2003: 19). Through status, some Nubians buried in Egypt could have shared much more with some Egyptians than with some Nubians in Nubia or the Egyptian Nile Valley (Budka, 2012: 52). It seems that in the first millennium BC, foreigners were considered to be those who were real incomers, bringing with them new ways of life, new languages, and names. Among these are numerous foreign mercenaries (Carians, Ionians, Phoenicians, Judeans, various Aramaic speaking groups) or representatives of foreign states governing Egypt for their kings residing somewhere else (Persians). Some of these people certainly stayed in Egypt and we know that they also adopted Egyptian names, titles, and at least some Egyptian customs (Vittmann, 2003). Yet, the descendants of all those people of foreign origin we know from previous periods lived next to these new foreigners as locals. The Egyptian umbrella term *ḫ3s.tjw* 'foreigners' is never used for peoples of foreign origin in an Egyptian sociocultural context. It was reserved for foreigners outside of Egypt (Schneider, 2010: 144).

This process of negotiation of Egyptiannes and otherness would repeat again under the Ptolemaic rule, from fourth to first century BC, when the main groups attested in the sources were Egyptians and Greeks (considered to be those who adhered to Hellenic culture). However, most people did not express their identity in such a binary way, and stressed their Egyptianess or Greekness to different extents depending on context (Winnicki, 1992). Greek art forms in Egypt were not reserved for 'Greeks', nor were Egyptian forms reserved for 'Egyptians' (Riggs, 2005: 22). Fiscal and cleruchic policies of the Ptolemies partially reshaped Egyptian society so that social status became preeminent and ethnicity no longer mattered to the state already before the Roman annexation (Fischer-Bovet, 2018). Again, we lose some of the groups from sight, such as previously mentioned foreign mercenaries. Some of them could have expressed their Egyptianness or Greekness more or even easier than others depending on their descent or cultural background.

After the Roman conquest of Egypt, these divisions and understandings of ethnic identity probably played far less a role than the status of citizen given by the Roman state (Riggs, 2005: 18). Romans were considered to be all who had legal status and rights of a Roman citizen, no matter the fact that they did not necessarily come from Rome or Europe or anywhere from the vast empire. J. Rowlandson has demonstrated that ethnic self-ascription is absent from Roman period documents from Egypt and even the ethnic labelling of the others is rare and not strictly ethnic (Rowlandson, 2013: 214). In the Roman period, many of the terms we consider ethnic also gained a legal connotation, so that Hellenes of the nome capital enjoyed the privilege of paying *laographia* (poll-tax) at a reduced rate (Goudriaan, 1988: 119).

After this short overview of over 3 millennia of ethnogenesis in ancient Egypt, the following sections will bring the reader closer to the problems of investigating ethnicity in the Nile Valley.

2 From Race to Culture and People: Egyptology of the Nineteenth and Early Twentieth Century

2.1 Egyptology and Scientific Racism

How early Egyptologists understood ancient Egyptians and their neighbours is nicely illustrated by a depiction from the tomb of King Seti I (1323–1279 BC) in the Valley of the Kings (Figure 1), which was discovered in 1817 by an Italian explorer, G. Battista Belzoni (1778–1823). The painted decoration of the tomb contains the depiction from the *Book of the Gates* (an ancient Egyptian funerary text) of what was then and is often even now referred to as the 'four races' (Figure 2). The depiction in question represents an Egyptian, a Nubian, a Libyan and a Syrian man using different colours for their skin according to the conventions in ancient Egyptian art (Section 1). These actually correspond to directions in the sky and are described in the accompanying text as 'cattle of god Re' (Quack, 2016: 291). They were interpreted by Egyptologists at the beginning of the discipline as 'four species: red, black, white and yellow' (Nott & Gliddon, 1854: 84), or in its developed phase as an expression of 'the universalist, super-racial conception of the world' (Bresciani, 1997: 225). This discovery fit well into the world views of Western Europeans during Belzoni's time. By then, the old division of humans into five races (Caucasian, Mongolid, Malay, Negroid and American), made by German physician, naturalist and anthropologist J. F. Blumenbach (1752–1840), in 1779, was already considered to be scientific fact (Gould, 1996: 402). Scientific racism mirrored the colonial world order with its hierarchy of races in which the white race was considered to be at the top and others races were judged and ordered by their degree of affiliation to it (Siapkas, 2014: 68). In order to prove this, early scholars turned to skeletal remains and the representations of ancient Egyptians and foreigners in ancient Egyptian art.

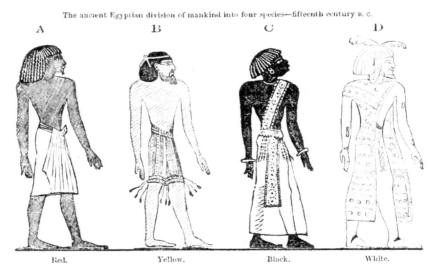

Figure 2 The so-called 'four races' depiction from the *Book of the Gates*
in the tomb of Seti I as interpreted by J. C. Nott & G. R. Gliddon
(redrawn after Nott & Gliddon, 1854: 85, fig. 1)

2.1.1 Craniometry

The use of craniometry (or the measurement of skulls), to study the racial
background of ancient and modern populations was a standard practice of the
nineteenth and early twentieth century. American physician and natural scien-
tist S. G. Morton (1799–1851) argued that the ranking of races could be
established objectively by physical characteristics and brain size (Gould,
1996: 83). Morton acquired cranial material from Egypt with the help of his
friend, English-born American G. R. Gliddon (1809–57), who was an
Egyptologist and US consul for Cairo (Morton, 1844: 1). Morton divided
the skulls into Caucasian, Negroid and Negro, with the Caucasian group
including Pelasgic, Semitic and Egyptian skulls. He supposedly found the
highest cranial capacity in the Pelasgic type (understood as Greek forebears),
and the lowest in the Negro type. Morton never considered that differences in
cranial capacity could be related to other factors, particularly body size and
sexual dimorphism. S. J. Gould calculated the cranial capacity again and
showed that, in Morton's sample, the male Negroid average is slightly
above the Caucasian male and the female Negroid average slightly lower
than the female Caucasian. Thus, differences in average cranial capacity
here record difference in stature due to sexual dimorphism, and not variations
in intelligence (Gould, 1996: 95).

Craniometry was also utilised by other, better-known Egyptologists. G. A. Reisner (1867–1942), an American archaeologist of Egypt, Sudan and Palestine, argued, based on craniometry, that the earliest population of Egypt and Nubia was racially and culturally identical, at least until the Second Cataract in Nubia (Reisner, 1910: 319; Reisner, 1923: 5). According to him, at the beginning of the third millennium BC, people beyond the First Cataract were less affected by cultural development in Egypt. This he explained with 'increasing change in the racial character of the people. The negroid element became more marked' (Reisner, 1923: 6). This demonstrates the inherent racism of Reisner, as, according to him, the increased presence of black people impeded the population beyond the First Cataract to culturally develop following the developments in Egypt.

English Egyptologist W. M. F. Petrie (1853–1942) collaborated with F. Galton (1822–1911) and K. Pearson (1857–1936), pioneers of eugenics, practice or advocacy of improving the human species by selectively mating people with specific desirable hereditary traits. Much like Gliddon sent crania to Morton, Petrie sent skeletal material from his excavations in Egypt to the University College in London Anthropometric Laboratory throughout his career (Challis, 2013; Challis, 2016). He also provided charts with cranial capacity for different 'races' (Figure 3).

Early scholars considered that there were two races living in the area of Thebes in Upper Egypt: Negroid and non-Negroid (Keith, 1906: 5). Petrie argued that differences in size and variability of skulls at the site of Naqada in

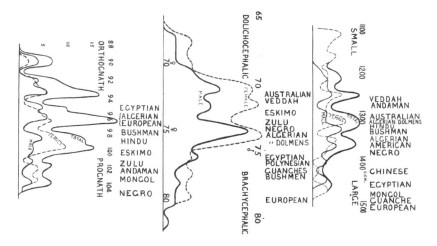

Figure 3 Cranial measures of different races according to W. M. F. Petrie
(redrawn after Petrie & Quibell, 1896: LXXXIV)

Upper Egypt indicate the arrival of a dynastic race superior to the inhabitants of the Nile Valley (Petrie & Quibell, 1896). According to British anthropologist D. E. Derry (1874–1961), the 'dynastic race' which built the pyramids came from the east (Derry, 1956: 81). He described it as: 'a dominant race, perhaps relatively few in numbers but greatly exceeding the original inhabitants in intelligence; a race which brought into Egypt the knowledge of building in stone, of sculpture, painting, reliefs, and above all writing; hence the enormous jump from the primitive Predynastic Egyptian to the advanced civilization of the Old Empire' (Derry, 1956: 85). The same opinion was held by British Egyptologist W. B. Emery (1902–1971) who distinguished between the 'Brown' or 'Mediterranean race', which was inhabiting Lower Nubia, and the 'Negroid race' living further south. He considered Lower Nubia and Upper Nubia to be distinct, both racially and culturally (Emery, 1965: 133–5). The idea of 'dynastic race' is the culmination of racist and colonial attitudes as at that time it was not imaginable that indigenous non-white populations could produce high culture.

2.1.2 The Hamitic Question

The concerns with racial differentiation in early archaeology of Egypt and Nubia were reflections of political views (contra Binder, 2019: 110). This is nicely demonstrated with the question of 'whiteness' of ancient Egyptians, known as the Hamitic question.

In the Bible, Ham is the son of Noah and the father of Cush (Nubian), Mizraim (Egyptian), Phut (Libyan) and Canaan. In the Old Testament, Ham is not attested as black, but the Babylonian Talmud, a collection of Jewish oral tradition from the sixth century AD, states that the sons of Ham were cursed by being black, which led to the idea established in the Middle Ages and continuing into eighteenth and nineteenth century, that black people were descendants of Ham (Foster, 1974: 177).

For early scholars of ancient Egypt it was very important to prove that ancient Egyptians belonged to the white race. Gliddon found it questionable that ancient Egyptians were the offspring of Ham, although this was the prevailing opinion of the time:

> For, if these unhappy descendants of Ham were under a curse, how was it, if Ham be the parent of the Egyptians, that these unfortunate people were the most civilized of antiquity? how was it, that this accursed race enjoyed, for 2500 years, the fairest portion of the earth? how came it that these unhappy people held the descendants of Shem in bondage, or in tribute, during 1000 years before Cambyse, B. C. 525? (Gliddon, 1843: 18)

For Gliddon, it was not imaginable that, as offspring of Ham, supposedly black Egyptians were the most civilised ancient people, having the dominion of the best part of the earth and even having Jews in bondage, according to the Biblical narrative. He referred to the Egyptian word Kush (Upper Nubia) as a barbarian country and a perverse race (Gliddon, 1843: 24), and added that 'civilization . . . could not spring from Negroes, or from Berbers, and NEVER DID' (Gliddon, 1843: 58, original emphasis). Consequently, the builders of the 'Ethiopian pyramids' (Meroitic pyramids in Sudan) were, according to Gliddon, a race foreign to Africa, namely white Caucasians (Gliddon, 1843: 59).

Particularly informative on racial prejudices of the time is Reisner's description of Lower Nubia during the first half of second millennium BC:

> I take my picture of the time largely from Lower Nubia as it is to-day, living its isolated, primitive agricultural life in political security, relying for its few luxuries on the sale of dates, goats, and basket-work, and on its income from servitors in the employment of Europeans. The population is now, I imagine, much the same in numbers, and much the same in culture, as it was then. The largest centres of population had then, as now, a few Egyptian officials, bullying the local inhabitants and cursing their place of exile . . . The imported objects were largely Egyptian-simple tools of copper, small alabaster vessels, wheel-made pots, blue-glazed beads and amulets, and perhaps certain kind of cloth; just as now one finds a few Egyptian pots, some European fabrics, petroleum tins, an occasional sewing-machine, porcelain vessels, and silver-plated spoons, the latter usually bearing the private marks of Cairo hotels! But the local culture, which has produced none of these things and is incapable of producing or even of fully utilising them, still remains practically late Neolithic in its conditions of life. I take it that a race which cannot produce or even fully utilise the products of a higher culture must, from an historical point of view, still be counted in its former state. The evidences of the fortuitous possession of the products of a higher culture only deepen the impression of cultural incompetence. (Reisner, 1923: 7)

This quote indicates that direct parallels between the colonialism of his time and ancient Egyptian domination in Nubia were not considered to be problematic for Reisner and his contemporaries. In fact, their experiences were their key to understanding the past because they considered that the population under foreign domination did not change, whether the colonisers were Egyptian or British.

J. H. Breasted (1865–1935), father of American Egyptology and founder of the Oriental Institute in Chicago, also shared the same racial ideas about mankind (Figure 4): 'If we look outside of the Great Northwest Quadrant, we find in the neighboring territory only two other clearly distinguished races – the

Figure 4 Distribution of different races in Europe and North
Africa according to J. H. Breasted
(redrawn after Breasted, 1935: 130; graphic A. Hassler, ÖAI/ÖAW)

Mongoloids on the east and the Negroes on the south. These peoples occupy an important place in the modern world, but they played no part in the rise of civilisation' (Breasted, 1935: 131).

Again we see that the reason behind insisting that ancient Egyptians belonged to the white race was the belief that other races cannot produce civilisations.

Austrian Egyptologist H. Junker (1877–1962) was a strong advocate of the idea that Africa was inhabited by Hamites (white race in Junker's work) and Negroes. According to him, the Negroes were dominated by a 'white' Hamitic superstratum (Matić, 2018a: 31). Junker disagreed with Reisner on the origin of Kerma culture in Nubia. He argued that its bearers were native Nubians, a highly developed African culture of the second millennium BC. According to Junker, Kerma was the only African high culture from the pre-Christian period which does not consciously lean on Egypt, like the Meroitic culture. The reason being that Junker considered that all cultures of the Nile Valley were produced by light-skinned Hamites and not dark-skinned Negroes (Matić, 2018a: 31). Where Reisner did not see Kerma as an indigenous Nubian culture because he interpreted Nubians as being racially different to Egyptians, Junker interpreted Kerma as an indigenous culture because he considered it to be Hamitic, which for him meant being white (Matić, 2018a: 39). Following the ideas of previous scholars such as Breasted and Junker, Emery also argued that the people of Kush were not 'Negroes, as we understand the term applied to this racial group today'. Instead he claimed that 'The Egyptians used the term "Negro" to designate all the dark-skinned peoples of the south, whatever their race' (Emery, 1965: 158). In this, he refers to the Egyptian term *Nḥs.y*, a generic term for southerners including both Egyptians and Nubians in Upper Egypt and Nubians south of the First Cataract.

Contrary to the ideas of these early scholars, anthropological research in the last few decades has demonstrated the similarity in morphometrical features between early third millennium BC Egyptians from Abydos and the population of Kerma in Upper Nubia. Studies of mitochondrial DNA suggest that modern Egyptians and Nubians are much more similar to one another than either is to the population of South Sudan (Williams, Belcher & Armelagos, 2005: 341). Whether or not ancient or modern Egyptians can be considered black depends on modern definitions of blackness. From a modern Egyptian frame of reference, far fewer ancient Egyptians would be categorised as black (Roth, 1998: 223). As we have seen in the case of M. Hefny (Section 1), even these frames of reference can change in another social context.

2.1.3 Scientific Racism and Ancient Egyptian Depictions of Foreigners

Authors such as Morton and Gliddon approached ancient Egyptian iconography as photographic verity (Kemp, 2018: 25). Morton compared Egyptian representations of women in fifteenth to eleventh century BC Theban tombs in Egypt to Nubian girls of his time (Morton, 1844: 24), and argued that Negroes were numerous in ancient Egypt, but that their social position was the same as in his time, that of servants and slaves (Morton, 1844: 66). Morton's ideas were welcomed in the American south where they were used to justify slavery (Gould, 1996: 101).

Nott and Gliddon even wrote:

> The monuments of Egypt prove, that Negro races have not, during 4000 years at least, been able to make one solitary step, in Negro-land, from their savage state; the modern experience of the United States and the West Indies confirms the teachings of monuments and of history; and our remarks on Crania, hereinafter, seem to render fugacious all probability of a brighter

future for these organically-inferior types, however sad the thought may be. (Nott & Gliddon, 1854: 95–6)

Comparing Egyptian representations of captive Nubians from New Kingdom monuments, they argued that they obtained proof that 'the Negro has remained unchanged in Africa, above Egypt, for 8,000 years; coupled with the fact that the same type, during some eight or ten generations of sojourn in the United States, is still preserved, despite of transplantation' (Nott & Gliddon, 1854: 249–50).

Petrie also used ancient Egyptian iconography for racial distinctions (Petrie, 1901: 250–4) and collected photographs of ancient Egyptian depictions of foreigners and organised them into racial groups (Petrie, 1887).

The distinctions between populations based on skin colour as depicted in ancient Egyptian art, a method going back to Morton, Gliddon, Nott and Petrie, are found also in later works. Thus, for American archaeologist B. Trigger (1937–2006), a difference in colour is an indication of the origin and conse- quently the status of depicted figures (Figure 5): 'The plantation scene in the tomb of the Nubian prince Djehutyhotep suggests that he may have been producing dates for export to Egypt. It is also possible that the distinction between black and brown skinned workmen in this scene is between Lower Nubians who worked as serfs on his estates and Negro slaves who came from farther south' (Trigger, 1976: 130).

Figure 5 Plantation scene from the tomb of Djehutyhotep, Debeira-East in Lower Nubia, reign of Hathspesut and Thutmose III, fifteenth century BC (digitally retouched after Säve-Söderbergh, 1987)

This quote nicely demonstrates that, although the term race is not used, the method of analysing depictions of Egyptians and foreigners in ancient Egyptian art remains the same as the one embedded in the racial approach. Differences in skin colour, namely brown or black, are taken as indicative of exact geographical origin and even status of the Nubians in question. The more black, the less free. The fallacy of this logic is demonstrated by numerous cases where Nubians depicted in both colours are described in the accompanying text as coming from the same region, indicating that the difference in colour is used as an optical effect. For example, Nubians depicted in the tomb of an Egyptian viceroy named Huy (Figure 11), which will be discussed further in Section 3, are depicted in both colours, although in the upper most register of the scene the text states that they come from Lower Nubia, and in the two lower registers the text states that they come from Upper Nubia. The optical effect is used in order to avoid visual blending of figures of the same colour; that is why black and brown figures alternate.

That ideas inherited from early Egyptology can find their way even into later scholarship is nicely illustrated also in a passage written by American Egyptologist D. B. Redford (1934–): 'One should never underestimate the overwhelming and irresistible attraction of the way of life of the triumphant imperial culture, whether Egyptian, Hellenic, Roman, or British. Something more than a grudging admiration had overcome Nubian chiefs such as Heka-nefer or Ruya: they had "realised" that to be Egyptian mean to be an Übermensch' (Redford, 2004: 10).

Much is revealed by this statement. Egypt, Greece, Rome and Britain are described as imperial cultures. Britain is placed at the end of a line of consecutive empires. Nubian chiefs are said to have realised that being Egyptian means to be *Übermensch*, a concept from the philosophy of F. Nietzsche who, in his book *Thus Spoke Zarathustra* (1883), refers to *Übermensch* as a goal which humanity is to set for itself. The context of Redford's sentence, and its structure, indicate that he understands *Übermensch* as something superior. This idea of *Übermensch* standing for a superior human was actually advocated by the Nazi regime, and such an understanding of Nietzsche's philosophy was used as the foundation for National Socialist ideas. Far from arguing that Redford's passage has a national socialist agenda, my point here is that one has to be more critical towards the terms used to describe certain phenomena. By utilising the concept of *Übermensch* to argue for the view of superiority of the Egyptians in the eyes of the Nubians, Redford may be unwillingly making associations to concepts and ideas tied to the racial superiority of one at the expense of other (Matić, 2018a: 37). Instead of claiming that Nubians, Hekanefer and Ruya realised that to be an Egyptian meant to be an *Übermensch*, we should consider that they probably aspired not to be just any Egyptian, but to be a high-status state official of Egypt. These are two considerably different things (Section 3).

One might find it incredible, but even the *British Museum Dictionary of Ancient Egypt* has an entry on race in which the authors state: '[the] apparently simple question of the racial origins or characteristic racial type of the Egyptians is both difficult to answer and in some measure irrelevant' (Shaw & Nicholson, 1995: 239). Irrelevant or not, the authors use the category of race as valid and further argue that 'examination of human remains from the Predynastic period shows a mixture of racial types, including negroid, Mediterranean and European, and by the time that Pharaonic civilization had fully emerged it was no longer meaningful to look for a particular Egyptian racial type, since they were clearly already, to some extent at least, a mixed population' (Shaw & Nicholson, 1995: 239).

What we can notice from this entry is not only that the category of race can find its way into a broadly distributed dictionary published by one of the most authoritative institutions in the field, but that the understanding of race does not substantially differ from that of the nineteenth century. The entry from the *British Museum Dictionary of Ancient Egypt* is unfortunately not an isolated example. I. Shaw writes in his chapter on ancient Egypt and the outside world in the *Oxford History of Ancient Egypt*, that anthropological studies suggest that the predynastic population of Egypt included 'a mixture of racial types (negroid, Mediterreanean and European)' (Shaw, 2000: 309). In her discussion on the connection between Punt and Harapan India, D. Michaux-Colombot even wrote that the ruler of Punt depicted in the temple of Hatshepsut in Deir el-Bahari (Figure 6) has Caucasian features understood as 'blond or flaxen haired' and being more in line with an 'Aryan immigrant in Pakistan than with a Sudanese' (Michaux-Colombot, 2004: 358). Problems with historical accuracy aside, a more urgent problem is the racial discourse involved and left unquestioned.

2.2 Egyptology, Culture-Historical Archaeology and Ethnic Identity

The increase in collected and excavated archaeological material in Europe, and a growing focus on its geographical distribution caused by nineteenth-century nationalist interest, slowly paved the way for a new archaeological paradigm – traditional or culture-historical archaeology (Trigger, 2008: 215). Archaeologists started to group together classes of objects, burials, dwellings, settlement organisations etc., among which they found similar traits. These were placed on distribution maps allowing for distinct archaeological groups or cultures to be defined (Lucy, 2005: 86). The old term race was slowly but

Figure 6 King and Queen of Punt, mortuary temple of Hatshepsut
in Deir el-Bahari, relief block from Egyptian Museum in Cairo
(photo, courtesy of Filip Taterka)

surely replaced with other terms such as people or ethnic group, but without any conceptual redefinition (Jones, 1997: 16; Saini, 2019: 95; Siapkas 2014: 69). There remained the concern with holism, homogeneity, order and boundedness (Jones, 1997: 48). Archaeologists working in Egypt and the Sudan at the end of the nineteenth and the beginning of the twentieth century predominantly had Western and Central European and American academic backgrounds. It is therefore not surprising that many of the ideas found in Western European and American archaeology of the time found their way into colonial archaeology in Egypt and Sudan. The following examples serve to illustrate this point.

Most of Petrie and Reisner's racial assumptions coloured their interpretation of the material culture. Petrie considered the Naqada culture with its core in Upper Egypt to be the product of the 'dynastic race'. Reisner coined the terms A, B and C-group for archaeological cultures of fourth and third millennium BC in Lower Nubia. The idea being that subsequent cultural groups follow one after the other and that development phases can be distinguished within each (e.g. ancient, classic and final A-group). Similarly, in Kerma in Upper Nubia another archaeological culture was defined and named after this site, also by Reisner.

Another Nubian archaeological culture was recognised by Petrie in cemetery X at Hu (Diaspolis Parva) in Upper Egypt in 1899 and named Pan-Grave culture after very shallow (sometimes less than 40 cm deep) circular pan-shaped graves, which later turned out to be a minority (de Souza, 2013: 109–10; Liszka, 2015: 43). In fact, the first example identified by Petrie as a Pan-Grave burial (Abadiyeh, grave E2) had grave contents distinctive for Kerma culture (de Souza, 2019: 7). M. Bietak argued that the Pan-Grave skeletons belonged to a 'Negroid race' and the C-group skeletons to a 'Europoid race'. Because of these racial differences, he assumed that the C-group people were indigenous inhabitants of the Nile Valley whereas Pan-Grave people had to come from elsewhere, and he suggested the Eastern Desert of Sudan (Bietak, 1966: 61–88). Thus, focus on race of the skeletons as the way to pinpoint their origin and movements went hand in hand with the culture-historical 'pots equal people' premise. Unfortunately, these race-centred interpretations are not reflected on even in the most recent study on Pan-Grave pottery (de Souza, 2019: 8). According to K. Lizka and D. Raue, these terms today cause more problems than solutions (Liszka, 2015: 49; Raue, 2019a: 293).

Culture-historical archaeologies often turn to those societies which have left written records in order to ethnically interpret those which did not. Culture-historical archaeologists search through the written sources for groups argued to have inhabited certain territories. In the next step they interpret archaeological cultures of these territories as material remains of groups they searched for in the written sources (Sherratt, 2005: 26). However, we cannot know whether historically documented ethnonyms were already being used in periods before they are attested in texts, nor if they had any value for those they are supposed to be naming (Chrisomalis & Trigger, 2003: 14). Continuity in name does not necessarily correspond to continuity in cultural practices and identities (Cruz, 2011: 337–40). Yet, Egyptologists more often than not seem to make such assumptions, as though ethnic identity was being simply inherited. We are warned about the fallacies of such assumptions from studies of more recent contexts, as, for example, what it meant to be Shona, BaKongo or Igba in Africa in the seventeenth century is not the same as today (Cruz, 2011: 352). The name of an ethnic group may stay the same, but the experience of being a member of this group may change; but also, the experience may stay relatively stable while the name can change (Jenkins, 2008: 171).

There are numerous examples for this from ancient Egypt. Here I would like to discuss three cases: 1. *Mḏ3.yw* – where an ethnonym from ancient Egyptian sources was used to label an archaeological culture which appears later and disappears earlier than the ethnonym; 2. Libyans – where similarity in ethnonyms is used to trace ethnicity backwards and label an entire region and its diverse population; and 3. Hyksos – where a term for the ruling class is used erroneously as an ethnonym to label an archaeological culture and the entire population of the Eastern Delta.

1.   The ancient Egyptian term *Mḏȝ.yw* (inhabitants of land or region *Mḏȝ* in the Eastern Desert) is often used for the population which produced and used the Pan-Grave culture (Baines, 1996: 376; Bietak, 1966: 61–78; Bietak, 2018: 74; Kemp, 2018: 40; Säve-Söderbergh, 1941: 138–40; Schneider, 2003: 82). The equation was first suggested by A. Weigall, a student of Petrie, in 1907 and later found in the works of T. Säve-Söderbergh, M. Bietak and others, rarely questioned even today. The argument used by a Weigall is a classic example of culture-historical 'pots equal people' premise. He based his equation on the Pan-Grave pottery found at the base of the ledge of the family shrine from fourteenth century BC at Gebel Agg in Lower Nubia where a man named Humay is depicted and has a title '*Mḏȝ.y* of His Majesty' (Liszka, 2015: 43–5).

Evidence for one group is then used to write historical narratives about the other (for criticism, see Liszka, 2015: 42). K. Liszka has shown that there are no solid arguments for interpreting *Mḏȝ.yw* and bearers of Pan-Grave culture solely as mercenaries, as often assumed, and that there is no Pan-Grave presence in the Eastern Desert, considered to be the land where *Mḏȝ.yw* lived. She suggests that Pan-Grave culture should rather be associated with the Nile Valley (Liszka, 2015: 42; see also de Souza, 2013: 109).

An additional problem is that a continuity in identity is silently argued through identification of modern Bedja with ancient Blemmies and ancient Egyptian *Mḏȝ.yw* (Zibelius-Chen, 2007: 391). Although most authors argue that from the sixteenth century BC onwards, *Mḏȝ.yw* did not signify an ethnic group but rather an occupation, D. Michaux-Colombot has been a vocal opponent of this idea, demonstrating the continuity of the use of the word *Mḏȝ.yw* even until Ptolemy III (284–222 BC), as Demotic Papyrus Lille 3, No. 99 mentions an entire village of the *Mḏȝ.yw* in the Fayum with men, women and children among them (Michaux-Colombot, 1994: 29). She even identifies the Meluhha from Akkadian cuneiform documents with the *Mḏȝ.yw* (Michaux-Colombot, 1994: 32; Michaux-Colombot, 2010). C. Rilly argues that *Mḏȝ.yw* are mentioned as enemies of Kush in late Napatan texts (fourth century BC) and probably also referred to in Meroitic texts (third century BC), and that Pliny the Elder in first century AD calls them Midoe or Midioe (Rilly, 2019: 132–3). The problem is that, in such identifications and arguments of ethnic continuity, the fact that none of these ethnonyms were explicitly used by the people or groups they are used to refer to by others (such as Egyptian, Greek or Roman authors) is not taken into account. Continuity in language is not the same as continuity in self-definition and ethnic identity.

A. Obłuski warned that, in the fifth century AD, the ethnonym Blemmyes was used to designate the population living in the Nile Valley which was ethnically not Blemmyan and therefore that the authors have erroneously attributed some elements of material culture to them (Obłuski, 2013).

The designation *Mḏ3.yw* could have changed meaning over several millennia. Authors advocating a *Mḏ3.yw* = Pan-Grave culture equation fail to explain the continuity of the term and discontinuity in the archaeological culture it supposedly referred to. Even in a recent study of the Pan-Grave pottery, it is suggested that the search for cultural connections may be extended both geographically, namely to C-group, Kerma culture, Jebel Mokram and Jebel Moya traditions, and chronologically, back to A-group and forward to Blemmyes and Beja tribes. Which cultural connections are supposed to be sought is not specified and terms such as 'group', 'culture' and 'tradition' are changed with a term 'horizon' which designates regional variants of the Pan-Grave culture (de Souza, 2019: 152). The underlying premise of culture-historical archaeology remains. Quite a complex term culture is reduced to techniques in manufacture and decoration of pottery.

2.   The same tracing of ethnicity backwards using an ethnonym is also found in the case of the Libyans. Phonetic similarities between the Egyptian word *Rbw* and Greek word *Libues*, the first being attested for the first time in thirteenth century BC Egypt and the second not predating the first millennium BC, are used to argue in favour of ethnic continuity (for criticism, see Cooney, 2011: 43). The term Libyan is a convention in Egyptology which actually denotes all non-Egyptians who lived in the region to the west of the Nile Valley and Delta (Snape, 2003: 94). Even in some recent studies, there seems to be no critical reflection on this matter. Rather, even the exalted position of women in Egypt during the rule of a Libyan dynasty at the beginning of first millennium BC is interpreted as possible Libyan influence. Evidence for this is sought both in the fifth century BC writings of Herodotus who reports on Libyan women going to war and riding chariots, or in the status of women among the Tuareg. The testimony of Herodotus is then used to interpret the information that, at the beginning of eleventh century BC, the mother of Payankh, high priest of Amun of Libyan descent, accompanied him on a campaign and assumed responsibility for many administrative duties (Becker, 2016: 39). The difference between Libyans of the thirteenth century BC, Libyans of first millennium BC, and Libyans described by Herodotus in fifth century BC and Tuareg are blurred simply because they all inhabited or inhabit regions west of Egypt we call Libya.

3.   An archaeological culture which has received increased scholarly attention in the recent years is related to the Hyksos kingdom in the Eastern Delta from

*c.*1650–1550 BC. Hyksos is a Greek term used by the first-century AD Jewish historian Josephus who recorded fragments of the writing of an Egyptian priest Manetho from early third century BC, which describe the conquerors from the east who invaded Egypt. The word Hyksos derives from Egyptian term *ḥḳȝ ḫȝs.wt* meaning 'ruler of hill-desert (foreign) lands'. Therefore, in the Egyptian language, it did not refer to an ethnic group, but was a title. In fact, ancient Egyptians themselves did not use this term for the rulers of foreign origin in the Eastern Delta, instead these rulers adopted the title themselves (Candelora, 2018: 47). Most Hyksos rulers had foreign names with northwest Semitic parallels possibly indicating a northwest Semitic origin (Schneider, 1998: 34, 150), but some of them like Khayan had both foreign and Egyptian names, and some like Apepi only Egyptian names. We should also bear in mind that not all Hyksos kings were outsiders although being of foreign origin. Some of them were born in Egypt (Roberts, 2013: 287). The scholarly consensus today is that these rulers of foreign origin used the opportunity provided by the weakened state and took control of the Eastern Delta.

Still, early scholars used the term Hyksos as a word for a race which supposedly invaded Egypt (Candelora, 2018) and, after increased excavations in the Eastern Delta, specifically at the site of Tell el-Dabᶜa (Avaris, ancient capital of the Hyksos) a specific archaeological culture was defined and slowly but surely the population which produced it was labelled Hyksos by Egyptologists (e.g. Bresciani, 1997: 234; Mourad, 2015; Redmount, 1995). In the Eastern Delta of that time, Syro-Palestinian burial customs, such as burying the dead within the settlement, burying an equid together with the deceased dignitary, and body of the deceased laid on the back with legs flexed, are found together with Egyptian burial customs (Bietak, 1996: 10–25; also Bader, 2011; Bader, 2013). New pottery style also developed in the region at the beginning of the Hyksos period (Bietak, Forstner-Müller & Mlinar, 2001: 172). This led to referring to the entire region as a kingdom ruled by and populated mostly by foreigners. Even in contemporary archaeology of Egypt, one may often find the adjective Hyksos to label a grave, cemetery, house, or settlement. In the process, a designation for a ruling class is transferred first onto all newcomers and then to the entire population of the eastern Delta (e.g. Haring, 2005: 171). Furthermore, depictions of 'Asiatics' in ancient Egyptian art are used as source of information for the ethnic features of the Hyksos (for criticism, see Cohen, 2015: 26). The past reality was, of course, much more complex (Bader, 2013). The population which inhabited this kingdom was surely diverse. However, Theban kings who controlled Upper Egypt in the south refer to their enemies in the north as Asiatics, no matter the diverse population of the region. They even depict these northern enemies of diverse origins as one unified group of foreigners in representations of the conflict, as evidenced by the depiction of the final war between king Ahmose from Thebes and the Hyksos kingdom in his Abydos temple from sixteenth century BC (Harvey, 1998). The problem emerges when Egyptologists confuse ancient Theban ideology with reality of the time (for criticism of this, see Polz, 1998) and consequently start seeing it in the archaeological record.

2.3 A Hidden Theory

Theory is, for example, in German archaeological publications, rarely found as a separate chapter or heading at the beginning of a paper or a monograph. It is more often than not implicit, or written between the lines (Rebay-Salisbury, 2011: 41–2). This implicit theoretical background shows itself only through interpretations and that is why it was termed 'hidden theory' by U. Sommer and A. Gramsch (2011: 25). However, this is not limited to German archaeology. Typical of the working of culture-historical reasoning as hidden theory is the use of archaeological cultures as a quasi ideology freely substitutes for ethnic groups without questioning the assumption that these correlate (Curta, 2014: 2510). Supposed pre-theoretical description of empirical evidence is nevertheless rooted in culture-historical reasoning which identifies ethnic identity behind it (Jones, 1997: 29). Several cases from Egyptology nicely illustrate this.

One of the typical cases of a culture-historical approach to material culture and ethnic identity is found in the interpretation of one cemetery from previously mentioned site Tell el-Dabᶜa. Some short time after the period of Hyksos rule in the place of an earlier palace, a cemetery was found in areas north of village ᶜEzbet Helmi. According to M. Bietak, the archaeological phase to which the cemetery belonged dates to the mid sixteenth century BC. However, this date of the stratum has been questioned (Höflmayer, 2018; Matić, 2018b). Judging by the published plan drawing, the cemetery contains twenty-eight graves, some of which involving multiple burials of individuals of varying age, among whom are also children (Figure 7).

According to both the drawings and the reports, the burials did not contain any grave goods. Yet, they were interpreted as burials of Nubian soldiers (e.g. Bietak, Dorner & Jánosi, 2001; for further references Matić, 2014a; Matić, 2018b), and this interpretation has rarely been questioned (Matić, 2014a). The arguments for this interpretation may be summarised as follows: some of the crania have Negroid elements and are therefore interpreted as Nubian; and handmade pottery of Nubian culture was found in other areas in Tell el-Dabᶜa, however not in these burials. A handful of supposedly Nubian silex arrowheads was found in area H/I of ᶜEzbet Helmi, however not in these burials, and are

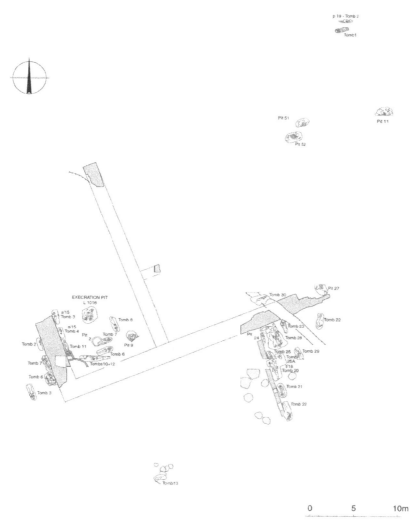

Figure 7 Plan of the cemetery in area ᶜEzbet Helmi, Tell el-Dabᶜa
(©ÖAI/ÖAW, redrawn after Bietak, Dorner & Jánosi, 2001: 70)

actually from a higher and thus unrelated archaeological layer. Finally, Theban
king Ahmose of mid sixteenth century BC had a military campaign in Nubia from
which he could have brought soldiers when he embarked against the Hyksos in
the north (for details see Matić, 2014a; Matić, 2018b). The problem with the last
argument is that it is based on the text of the autobiography of Ahmose son of
Ebana, who was a soldier in service of Ahmose. He actually states in the
autobiography that the campaign in Nubia occurred after the campaign against
Avaris (Matić, 2014a). In the same cemetery, two supposedly non-funerary pits

were also found with skeletal remains of individuals who were interpreted as Nubian using the same arguments as those for the interpretation of the rest of the cemetery population (Matić, 2018b).

What we are observing in the example of the Tell el-Dabᶜa cemetery and execration pits, is the combination of several key points discussed in this section, namely, pottery as remains of a specific ethnic group and skulls as keys for racial identification, and therefore also ethnic attribution of skeletal remains. These arguments are quintessential features of culture-historical reasoning in archaeology.

That culture-historical assumptions on the equation material culture=people can be combined with other problematic assumptions such as the quality of production as a reflection of ethnicity is clear from C. Hubschmann's search for the Libyans in the archaeological record. The simple argument behind this search can be summarised as follows. Libyans are depicted bringing ostrich eggs and feathers in Egyptian fifteenth to eleventh century BC art and wearing ostrich feathers on their heads, therefore the presence of undecorated ostrich eggshell fragments found in all levels of occupation at Bates' Island should suggest Libyan presence. The same was argued for the fort at Zawiyet Umm el-Rakham, where additional features have been interpreted as Libyan. Namely, several circular stone structures within the fort lack plaster and grey/black coarse ware pottery and sherds made of local fabric with shell inclusions were found on the floor level around the circular structures (Hubschmann, 2010: 176–7). The author writes that the crude manner of the construction of these structures 'makes it doubtful that they were manufactured by Egyptians or used for trade; they were most likely made by local inhabitants for utilitarian purposes' (Hubschmann, 2010: 178). It is assumed that Egyptians do not construct or use crude structures for utilitarian purposes. However, it seems that both Egyptians and Libyans inhabited the fortress of Zawiyet Umm el-Rakham and cooperated with each other (Snape, 2003: 103–4). In such a context, people of different origins and identities could have used material culture from different traditions, and therefore a search for clear divisions is blurring the reality of daily life at the site.

Sometimes different cultural elements can be found in the same context, demonstrating the limits of premises of culture-historical archaeology. For example, M. R. Buzon argues that four burials from Tombos were identified as Nubian based on both Nubian burial ritual (flexed position on the side) and because a Nubian bowl was found at the head of two women 'providing additional evidence of Nubian ethnicity' (Buzon, 2006: 688; Buzon, 2008: 173). However, apart from these bowls, the grave goods associated with all four burials were otherwise Egyptian (Smith, 2007: 237). Flexed position in burials sometimes associated with funerary beds and Nubian pottery appears in New Kingdom tombs at Aniba, Tombos and Soleb (Spencer, Stevens & Binder, 2017: 45). This makes one wonder whether the flexed position of these individuals is more an expression of specific funerary customs. When the burials contain material culture of both Egyptian and Nubian provenance how do we discern which of these had more value or meaning in defining identity? Were these Nubian women buried with Egyptian grave goods, or women of Nubian descent, but aspiring to Egyptian identity while being buried according to Nubian funerary beliefs? Are the terms Egyptian and Nubian adequate here?

Culture-historical understanding of material culture and identity also fails in addressing the dynamic processes behind static archaeological record. For example, M. Bietak has recently attempted to identify separate Egyptian and Asiatic communities in Tell el-Dab°a at °Ezbet Rushdi III, where an administrative quarter of the town dating to eighteenth to seventeenth century BC was found (Figure 8). Namely, in the excavated area, large houses with courtyards were found and two long north-south oriented streets divide at least three quarters. The one in the very west was interpreted as administrative, because of the numerous seal impressions found there, whereas those in the east as domestic, because of significantly lower numbers of these seal impressions.

Figure 8 Plan of the settlement in area °Ezbet Rushdi III, Tell el-Dab°a
(©ÖAI/ÖAW, courtesy of I. Forstner-Müller)

Bietak noticed that toggle pins were also found in the eastern quarters and that intramural burials are largely lacking at the site, being present in a small number in the two eastern blocks. Arguing that the Hyksos employed Egyptians in their administration and that toggle pins and intramural burials are an 'Asiatic' ethnic marker in Egyptological sence, he postulated that Egyptians lived in the western administrative quarter and Asiatics or Egyptianised Asiatics in the two eastern quarters. Consequently, he rejects the interpretation of the western quarter as administrative, because of the lack of systematically constructed units (Bietak, 2016: 270).

The problem with Bietak's interpretation is that there are hardly any original floors and the finds could therefore belong to the previous building phase, which Bietak has indeed acknowledged. However, for him this does not pose a problem, because this would not change the conclusion based on distribution patterns, as he argues that previous phases led to the final settlement situation (Bietak, 2016: 270). He does not take into account the temporal component, for when we consider the number of the pins, and the fact that they could have also been distributed chronologically as well as spatially, the overall distribution map changes considerably. The area was settled throughout eighteenth and seventeenth and re-used in the late sixteenth century BC. Therefore, if there were only one to several pins in one chronological phase of the site Bietak would probably not draw the same conclusion. Toggle pins are also known in Egypt from Tell el-Maskhuta, Tell el-Yehudiyeh, Tell Heboua, Kom Rabia, and Gurob, sites concentrated in Eastern Delta or adjacent Lower Egyptian regions. While some view these as good indicators of Canaanite presence (Sparks, 2004: 34), their distribution in Egypt could also indicate specific north Egyptian openness to dress elements of Canaanite origin. Culture-historical archaeology functioning as hidden theory silently assumes that the explanation can only be sought in terms of ethnicity. The possibility of a distinct taste or habitus is not taken into consideration. The next section demonstrates the complexity behind material expressions of ethnic identity.

3 Ethnic Identity: Recent Perspectives in Egyptology

Processual archaeologists during the 1960–70s challenged culture-historical understanding of material culture. They insisted on logical positivism, formation and testing of hypothesis, building models, and turning to anthropology and hard science in the epistemological background of their research. Culture was under-stood as a specific extra-somatic adaptive mechanism. Ethnicity was not on the agenda and culture-historical archaeology, which almost exclusively focused on this, was considered to be an outmoded archaeological paradigm (Jones, 1997: 5;

Lucy, 2005: 91; Roberts & Vander Linden, 2011: 1). In the process, questions of identity in the past were largely neglected and although attention was given to different research questions, archaeological cultures were still used.

The growing insistence of postprocessual archaeologists in the 1980s and 1990s on the meanings of things, has led to arguing that material culture does not simply passively reflect ethnic identity, but is an active element in its negotiation (Curta, 2014: 2509; Lucy, 2005: 102; Voss, 2008: 12). Social groups are not the same as things (Jenkins, 2008: 169). Material culture is what we have left of them and it is not the same as representatives of an ethnic group interviewed by ethnographers (Normark, 2004: 111–12). Some ethnic identities, like that of the Banda in Ghana, are based on intangible cultural practices that do not leave imprints on the archaeological record (Cruz, 2011: 345). As early as the 1980s, it has been demonstrated that there is no one-to-one correlation between a stylistic group (equivalent to archaeological culture) and an ethnic group (Hodder, 1982). If and which forms of material culture can be used to express any kind of identity is not something we can assume before analysis. For example, as we have seen in the previous section, pottery is more often than not used to define archaeological cultures which are then interpreted as material remains of ethnic groups, but there are enough examples showing that in some societies this is not the case. Thus, ceramics produced in the Banda area of west-central Ghana during the nineteenth and twentieth century lack ethnic connotations (Cruz, 2011).

In the last several decades, diverse approaches to ethnic identity and ethnicity appeared in sociology, anthropology, and consequently archaeology. I will shortly discuss these current approaches providing illustrative case studies on ancient Egypt to better explain them.

3.1 Primordial Approach

The understanding of ethnic identity as primordial gives group members a deep-rooted psychological sense of identity. Ethnicity is, in this approach, something deeply embedded, immutable, and prior to all other social relations. This approach argues that primordial bonds between individuals result from the givens of birth, such as blood, language, religion, territory, and culture, which can be distinguished from other social ties on the basis of the importance of the tie itself (Jones, 1997: 65). In a way, a primordial understanding of ethnicity reiterates the essentialism of racial theories because, according to this approach, ethnicity is biologically hereditary, as ethnic identity is based on attachments acquired at birth (Section 2). The focus of primordialists was to define the cultural repertoire of an ethnic group (Siapkas, 2014: 66–8). However, human groups cannot be reduced to folkloric repositories of distinctive values and cultural attributes (Moreno García, 2018: 2). A further problem with this approach is that it argues that cultural traits which form ethnic groups are fixed and involuntarily (Jones, 1997: 69). We have seen that these have often changed in ancient Egyptian history (Section 1). This approach is therefore very close to culture-historical archaeology and, as we have seen in Section 2, it is the most commonly encountered understanding of ethnic identity utilised in interpretations of ancient Egypt.

3.2 Instrumentalist Approach

The instrumentalist approach conceptualises ethnicity as a sociopolitical vehicle mobilised in certain situations in order to maximise the interests of an individual or a group (Siapkas, 2014: 70). Instrumentalists see ethnic identity as dynamic and situational, embedded in the organisation of social behaviour and the institutional fabric of society (Jones, 1997: 72). Such an understanding of ethnic identity gives group members motivation towards a certain end, linked to existence and continuity, so that they can change their ethnic identity for beneficial reasons (Normark, 2004: 133).

Norwegian anthropologist F. Barth (1928–2016) was most influential in the formation of this approach to ethnic identity. In his ethnographic work in Kurdistan, he focused on ethnicity as an individualising strategy and argued against ethnic identity as a simple list of traits (dress, food, language, blood, and culture) and stressed the importance of spatial, notional, and ideological boundaries for these features. According to Barth, ethnic identity is fluid and mutable. To have ethnic identity means to do things in a certain way (Barth, 1969: 119). Therefore, following Barth, ethnicity is not the same as culture; it is a marker of the social border (Cornell, 2004: 70). According to T. D. Hall, although primordial and instrumental approaches are often understood as mutually opposite, they are in fact poles of a continuum. The key difference is timescale, as ethnicity appears primordial, where the social processes that construct ethnicity take place over many generations, but when the processes occur over years or decades, social construction becomes more obvious (Hall, 2014: 52). The long history of the ancient Egyptian state and rich sources allow us a unique opportunity to study both cases.

Only some Egyptologists explicitly adopted Barth's ideas. In the previous section, I have discussed the case of tracing ethnicity backwards using ethonyms in the case of the Libyans with all associated problems of such an approach. In contrarst, E. M. Cole discusses evidence for the continuation of Libyan identity in Egypt, arguing that according to Barth, ethnic identities can be preserved if there are persisting cultural differences (Cole, 2015: 114).

However, Cole further argues that he understands markers of ethnic groups as demonstrating cultural differences between the Libyan and the Egyptian ethnic and cultural identity (Cole, 2015: 114). It is unclear on what basis he assumes that ethnic and cultural identity are the same and which arguments he uses to identify certain traits as ethnic rather than anything else. As I. Hodder has demonstrated through his research in Kenya, 'cultures did not always equal ethnic units' (Hodder, 1982: 11). According to Cole, the fact that Libyans were keen on using Libyan rather than adopting Egyptian names like other foreigners, indicates that naming was a cultural marker of Libyan ethnicity (Cole, 2015: 115). In Section 1, I have mentioned examples which contradict this; among others, wives of Thutmose III buried as elite Egyptian women kept their foreign names. The problem with Cole's equation is that there is no simple and rigid one-to-one relationship between ethnic groups and cultural similarities or differences. Since not all traits are relevant for ethnic identity and cultural traits end over time, also ethnic traits could change over time (Johnson, 1999: 212). The crucial question is instead where does culture end and ethnicity begin (Saini, 2019: 42). People of Libyan descent in the first millennium BC were not less local because of their choice of Libyan names and not as foreign as foreigners living outside Egypt. Keeping Libyan names could have been a mechanism for tracing lineage, strengthening kinship, and claim to a territory, rather than sending a deliberate message of being foreign and different.

Glimpses of instrumentalist postulates are possibly seen in the approach of several authors to the inhabitants of the Eastern Delta in the first half of the second millennium BC. The formation of specific Eastern Delta pottery tradition during the Hyksos period at Tell el-Dab^{c}a in the seventeenth and sixteenth centuries BC (Bietak, Forstner-Müller & Mlinar, 2001: 172) is even seen as an example of an ethnic group as a self-defining system (Haring, 2005: 171). According to I. Hodder, more marked differences in material culture of different ethnic groups emerge in moments of great tension or stress, such as competition over resources (Hodder, 1982: 35). The Hyksos kingdom in this region had a competitive neighbour (for land and resources), the Theban kingdom in the south. As was mentioned in the previous section, the Hyksos rulers were of foreign origin, so it is interesting to consider the possibility that changes in burial customs could have been a reflection of aspiring to certain practices of the ruling class and other co-inhabitants of the region with foreign origin. D. Arnold states that 'growing involvement with regions beyond the frontiers created a more intricate complex of relationships that not only changed the Delta inhabitants' material culture and way of life, but also have influenced people's self-understanding in fundamental ways' (Arnold, 2010: 185). In a way, Arnold's understanding of the processes occurring in the Eastern Delta during the Hyksos rule is also close to the approach to ethnic identity as emerging from the shared habitus, as will be discussed.

One possible example of an instrumentalist approach may be found in K. Liszka's study of the *Mḏ3.yw* (also see Section 2). She argues that pastoral nomads had been living for a while in the Eastern Desert of Egypt, not as politically unified but diverse groups, and then asks when did these people adopt the ethnic identity of the *Mḏ3.yw* as constructed by the Egyptians? (Liszka, 2011: 154). Prior to the late sixteenth century BC, Egyptian sources seem to show a certain ambiguity towards the knowledge of the land of Eastern Desert around the First and the Second Cataract and its inhabitants. *Mḏ3* seems to be a generic term signifying 'ideologically constructed location southeast or east of Egypt' (Liszka, 2011: 158). Administrative texts and execration texts (a form of curses) seem to put more emphasis on very specific toponyms in this region, each with a prince and delivering tribute. According to Liszka, this indicates that we are dealing with several entities which do not have to share common group identity nor be politically uniform. In fact, Liszka has shown that those individuals who most probably had origin in the Eastern Desert preferred to identify themselves as *Nḥs.y*, a term which was used generally for southerners (Michaux-Colombot, 2014: 508–9). She also demonstrated that sometimes the term *Mḏ3.yw* is understood as belonging to the *Nḥs.y* and sometimes the two terms are kept apart. Bearing in mind that both terms are Egyptian, and the fact that even for Egyptians sometimes their differences were not so strong, indicates that the people they described with those terms probably did not see themselves in the same way. However, C. Rilly managed to demonstrate that there was a difference in *Mḏ3.yw* and Kushite language and therefore argued that the difference between a *Mḏ3.y* and a *Nḥs.y* was not only geographical and sociological, but also linguistic (Rilly, 2019: 132). We should not exclude the possibility that the Egyptians used one term for several different groups which did not necessarily share one common language.

More aggressive Egyptian policy towards Lower Nubia during the nineteenth century BC, building the military fortresses in this region and controlling the movement of the people Egyptians described as *Nḥs.y*, could have encouraged people of the Eastern Desert to identify as *Mḏ3.yw*. In a political context in which identifying as *Nḥs.y* to Egyptians could do more harm than good, *Mḏ3.yw* seems to be a convenient solution. This process of appropriation of a stereotypical term coined by Egyptians by the people of the Eastern Desert is, according to Liszka, related to the ethnogenesis of *Mḏ3.yw*. Ethnogenesis refers to the formation of new cultural identities through historical and cultural shifts that make previous kinds of identification less relevant, giving rise to new forms of identity (Voss, 2008: 1). It can be intertwined with the formation of a political community and it tends to occur at frontiers and borderlands, especially in time of conflict and rupture (Hu, 2013: 391–4). Liszka argued that the meaning of the word *Mḏ3.yw* shifted again after the sixteenth century BC, when those who now identified themselves as *Mḏ3.yw* fought on the side of the Theban kings against the Hyksos. Their reputation caused the term to slowly but surely acquire a meaning of police, and later on any skilled person could be called a *Mḏ3.y* no matter their ethnic background (Liszka, 2011: 163–7). The idea that the *Mḏ3.yw* lost ethnic connotation during the New Kingdom was first proposed by W. M. Müller in 1910 and then elaborated by A. H. Gardiner in 1947 and G. Posener in 1958. K. Liszka convincingly argues that, contrary to some doubts, the *Mḏ3.yw* are in the *Onomasticon of Amenope*, a text from the beginning of eleventh century BC, an occupation (specialised police forces protecting the royal tombs) rather than an ethnic group (Liszka, 2010: 315–19). In fact, the title 'leader of *Mḏ3.yw*' in the period between fifteenth and eleventh century BC seems to be more attested with office bearers having Egyptian names (Olsen, 2013: 145). But this does not necessarily mean that their descent is not foreign. Most sources of this period indicate that the *Mḏ3.yw* had the role of intermediaries and not of police, as often assumed (Olsen, 2013: 155). Liszka warns us that her conclusion is still based on Egyptian sources which could have quite distorted the ancient reality. Her analysis is nuanced, yet one has to stress that the number of those who identify themselves as *Mḏ3.yw* during the nineteenth century BC is rather small. Her study nicely demonstrated the shifts in meaning of a toponym and an ethnonym, and how it could be instrumentalised by some for their own benefits in certain historical contexts. Namely, events on one periphery, Lower Nubia, caused changes in relation to Egyptians in the other periphery (Eastern Desert).

A similar case of instrumentalist understanding of ethnicity is found in the work of M. R. Buzon on Tombos. She argues that local Nubians could have adopted Egyptian identity starting from the sixteenth century BC because of its advantages (Buzon, 2008: 177). She argues that being a member of Egyptian society meant having less violent experiences during one's lifetime, and assumes that Kerma during the eighteenth to sixteenth century BC was a 'culture of violence' (Buzon, 2008: 180). However, although Buzon builds her argument of a less violent Egyptian society in Nubia based on skeletal evidence of trauma, she neglects numerous Egyptian textual and visual sources indicating just how violent Egyptian society could also be (Bestock, 2018; Matić, 2019).

The problem one faces with an instrumentalist approach is the degree to which instrumentalist adoption of certain cultural traits or practices is indicative of changes in ethnic identity. One good example is the use of Egyptian script and iconography by the rulers of Kerma to project their power over their new subjects in Lower Nubia starting from the seventeenth century BC. These subjects included both local Nubians and Egyptian settlers who inhabited previously Egyptian-governed military fortresses (Cooper, 2018). Rather than seeing the use of Egyptian script and iconography as a change in expression of Kushite ethnic identity, we should see this as a mechanism of exercising power in a manner recognisable by a desired audience.

3.3 *Topos* and *Mimesis*: A Structuralist Approach

A specific approach to foreigners as depicted in ancient Egyptian texts has been developed in Egyptology on the basis of structuralism; a linguistic, social, and anthropological theory arguing that cultural elements must be understood through their relationship to a broader system. A. Loprieno uses two concepts in his analysis of foreigners in ancient Egyptian literature, *topos* and *mimesis*. According to Loprieno, *topos* is characterised by semantic elements such as +foreign+people-*m3ᶜ.t* (ancient Egyptian concept of order) and is found in wisdom literature and royal discourse, whereas *mimesis* is characterised by semantic elements such as +foreign+*rmṯ* (humans)+name and is found in royal discourse and narrative literature (Loprieno, 1988: 15).

According to his formula, foreigners are not human (Loprieno, 1988: 22) which actually cannot be confirmed by Egyptian sources (Moers, 2005). Furthermore, whereas mimetic foreigners in literature are named, come forth as individuals, have speaking capacity and human appearance, topic foreigners are ethnically connotated, do not have speaking capacity, and have unhuman appearance (Loprieno, 1988: 44). These concepts, developed by Loprieno, were adopted by other Egyptologists. S. T. Smith uses these concepts 'to contrast the creation and deployment of ethnic stereotypes in the state ideology with the more nuanced and fluid depiction of ethnicity in more prosaic texts and personal monuments' (Smith, 2007: 220). According to T. Schneider, *topos* is society's official and normative perception, and *mimesis* a narrative attempt to portray foreigners as valuable individuals (Schneider, 2010: 147). A. D. Espinel argues that official or canonical, stereotypical representations of the third millennium BC fall under the category *topos*, whereas the profane, private, or daily sphere and its representation fall under the category *mimesis*, 'a sphere where the interpretation of reality has not passed through the filter of the mythical perspective'. According to Espinel, *mimesis* reveals an Egyptian view of reality linked to daily nature and stressed that the dividing line is not as clear as one would expect (Espinel, 2006: 446). However, the crucial idea of

Loprieno that both *topos* and *mimesis* are literally constructs is missed. They are not a direct reflection of reality or daily experiences with foreigners, which were surely as diverse as ancient Egyptian society itself.

This structuralist approach to ancient Egyptian texts describing foreigners or images depicting them, although useful in understanding their ideological background, helps us little in understanding the dynamic processes behind ethnic constructions and identifications.

3.4 Egyptianness and Foreignness: Habitus and Ethnic Identity

The concept of habitus (for definition, see Section 1) is used to bridge the polarisation of primordialist and instrumentalist views of ethnicity and to comprehend their relationship to culture (Skiapas, 2014: 72). Although a fairly well-known concept in other historical fields and archaeologies (Schreg et al., 2013: 109), less has been written on its use in Egyptology.

S. T. Smith is one of the rare Egyptologists who has used the concept of habitus in his research. He argued that the tension between individuals and habitus is particularly heightened in situations of cultural contact, such as the case with Egyptians in Nubia (Smith, 2014: 195). In several of his studies he argues that the steady increase of Nubian pots in an Egyptian fortress at Askut in Nubia, and thus presumably Nubian cuisine over time, implies that this phenomenon is not just a passive retention of a Nubian habitus, but an active assertion of Nubian ethnic identity that eventually managed to dominate (Smith, 2003b: 193–205; Smith, 2007: 234; Smith, 2014: 204). In his latest work, Smith argues that the use of cooking pottery could be an example of the reflection of habitus of Nubian women within the colony (Smith, 2018: 136). There are several related problems which have to be considered.

First is the assumption of direct correlation between Nubian pots, cuisine, and ethnic identity. Second is the assumption that the increased use of Nubian pots, and presumably preference for Nubian cuisine, reflects increased presence of Nubian identity, however this presence is understood, as the physical presence of Nubians or a change in the identity of the Egyptians stationed in military fortresses in Lower Nubia. There is also an equally valid possibility that this increase in Nubian pots rather reflects changes in taste and preference for either these vessels, or the food which was, or could be, prepared or served using them. This change does not necessarily reflect a change in ethnic identity, but rather the change in habitus. For example, C. Walsh has demonstrated that the contexts of Kerma pottery from Egypt during the first half of second millennium BC do not necessarily point to Kerman identity or origin for its users, but rather to shared tastes, at least among some, because only specific vessel forms (beakers) were being used in Egypt (Walsh, 2018: 43; for similar arguments for sixteenth and fifteenth century BC Egypt, see Raue, 2019b: 578). One should also consider the possibility that shared culinary practices can minimise rather than highlight difference (Voss, 2008: 250). An approach more in line with the concept of habitus would be to understand these changes as something that even those who were affected by them did not notice themselves. These changes slowly but surely became part of what they did, but they did not necessarily become part of who they were. One does not need to confine analysis within geographical areas or ethnic communities, but can discuss the frequency and extent of certain practices over time and space independently of their assumed cultural origins (Cornell & Fahlander, 2007: 8).

The third problem with Smith's interpretation is the one concerning gender. Namely, Smith assumes that cooking was an activity of women and that therefore the presence of Nubian cooking pots indicates not only physical presence of Nubian women, but also that they married Egyptian soldiers (Smith, 2003a: 56–7). Similarly, B. Bader relates the presence (2.5 per cent) of hand-made imported flat-based cooking pots, common in the southern part of Syria-Palestine, at Tell el-Dabᶜa as evidence for the presence of women with a Syro-Palestinian cultural background (Bader, 2011: 64–5). E. Pappa has rightly emphasised that such a binary gender pattern behind archaeological interpretations of actors in contact zones repeats quite often and reflects stereo-typical colonial gender assumptions, regardless of the studied context (Pappa, 2013). Whether one finds oneself in Askut in Nubia or in ancient Avaris in the eastern Delta (Bietak, 2016: 265), it is always the settler men, often interpreted as warriors or soldiers, who marry local women. Pappa argues that such colonial models cannot be a priori taken without proper investigation.

Smith assumes that there were no women in the Egyptian fortresses in Lower Nubia and he also assumes that stationed men, soldiers or others, needed women to do the cooking, because in Egyptian society cooking was usually associated with women in the textual and iconographic record. However, we are clearly dealing with different contexts and one cannot exclude that in military forts men took on themselves some activities which they could have been less associated with in other contexts. Furthermore, although maybe not attested at the Askut fortress, women were surely also inhabitants of other Egyptian fortresses in Lower Nubia, as possibly evidenced by a sealing from Mirgissa (Room 47) belonging to a woman, 'lady of the house', named Nebet-Kepeny or Lady of Byblos (Mourad, 2017: 388). When Tell el-Dabᶜa and presence of foreign women is concerned, although being recently confirmed based on isotope analyses (see Section 4 for details), this does not mean that only Syro-Palestinian women were associated with the use of handmade cooking pots as assumed by Bader.

Most recently, K. Liszka uses habitus as a tool in her study of dry-stone architecture at Wadi el-Hudi, el-Hisnein, and Dihmit, sites related to early second millennium BC mining activity in the Eastern Desert. She argues that the different building traditions of Egyptians (mudbrick) and dry-stone (Nubians) reflect a different habitus in each case. Comparison with Nubian architecture from the Nubian site Wadi es-Sebua allowed her to trace Nubian building techniques at Egyptian mining sites and argue that Nubians were involved in building the structures for Egyptians, as the structures have Egyptian design (Liszka, 2017: 6–7). She reinforces her interpretation by referring to an inscription from Wadi el-Hudi in which the Egyptian steward Intef, son of Pashedu, mentions that he brought with him all the *Nḥs.y* of Wawat (Lower Nubia), Sety (Upper Egypt?), and south and north (Liszka, 2017: 11). The problem is that as much as this example nicely demonstrates the proper understanding of the concept of habitus, it does not clearly demonstrate its connection to ethnicity. For example, K. Liszka argues that habitus can become an ethnic marker when contrasting forms of behaviour are juxtaposed from two different cultures (Liszka, 2017: 7), but apart from identifying Nubian presence based on building tradition (dry-stone architecture), written sources, and Nubian pottery, she does not use the idea that difference in habitus can become an ethnic marker. In fact, the written sources she quotes indicate that the Nubians presumably employed as builders were already considered to be foreign. Egyptians and Nubians did not have to juxtapose their building traditions to recognise each other as being different. Their native languages were different, so were their customs, cuisine, etc.

3.5 Postcolonial Theory and Ethnic Identity

Colonisation can be most broadly defined as 'appropriation of a previously autonomous region and its transformation into a dependency under the control of a remote entity' (Voss, 2008: 2). Defined like this, colonisation is a concept applicable to different cases of the expansion of ancient Egyptian state and settling of Egyptians to various degrees in neighbouring territories (for different imperial and colonial models see Smith, 1991). However, colonialism is a much broader concept in which the coloniser and the colonised are in an asymmetrical power relationship in which the coloniser is argued to be more advanced and therefore the dominant force in the relationship. Unlike, colonisation, colonialism is much more difficult to apply in cases of ancient Egyptian relationships to populations in newly conquered lands. As we have seen in Section 2, early scholars did not find it problematic to interpret the past based on their own colonial experiences in the present. The reason for this is the racist assumption that colonised populations, being racially impeded, do not and cannot change.

The complex and divergent field of postcolonial studies and postcolonial theory had made a major impact on archaeology since the 1990s. Unlike colonialism, postcolonial theory brings back agency to the colonised and argues that colonial experience changes the coloniser as much as the colonised. Just like the instrumentalist approach to ethnic identity, it argues against the essentialist notion of identity and puts focus on complex phenomena of social encounter and interaction, and on all of its unpredictable consequences. The works of postcolonial scholars such as E. Said (1935–2003) and G. Ch. Spivak (1942–) influenced revisions of nineteenth- and twentieth-century scholarship and the way archaeologists, historians, and art historians study one cultures' representations of other cultures. Whereas Said stressed that the way the Western world perceives the East is rooted in a long tradition of false romanticised images and discoursive strategies he terms *orientalism* (Said, 1978), Spivak asks if the subaltern, colonial populations who are socially, politically, and geographically outside the hierarchy of power, can even speak? (Spivak, 1998). She argues that the white male Western academic thinking is produced in order to support Western economical interests. Speaking in the name of the subaltern should not be confused with actual subaltern experiences. In the case of ancient Egypt, these ideas become clear when one bears in mind that we are more often than not confronted with ancient Egyptian representations of the foreigners and that when foreigners in ancient Egyptian contexts depict themselves, they do so using ancient Egyptian patterns of representation (Section 1).

Three main theoretical concepts coming from the work of H. Bhabha (1949–), one of the most quoted postcolonial theorists, are often found in recent archaeological works: hybridism, mimicry, and third space (Matić, 2017). For each of the terms, I will first discuss their meaning within postcolonial theory and then their usage in archaeology more broadly and Egyptology specifically. Numerous recent archaeological and Egyptological studies in which a reference to Bhabha's work is provided without clear implication on the study cannot be covered here.

3.5.1 Hybridism

Hybrid, in postcolonial theory, is a subject inhabiting an in-between reality and questioning the images and presence of authority (Bhabha, 1994: 13–113). According to H. Bhabha, all social collectives, nation states, cultures, and small-scale ethnic groups are caught in continuous processes of hybridity. He argued that encounters result in something new and substantially different than just conglomerates of new and old elements, because hybridity is not a problem of genealogy or identity between two cultures (Bhabha, 1994: 114). Yet, if following Bhabha, no culture is pure and each is a hybrid, then hybridity becomes a redundant term with limited use as a conceptual tool. The very use of the terms Myceanean, Roman, or Asian means accepting the existence of something pure (Stockhammer, 2013: 12–13). How similar were Myceaneans living in continental Greece to those living outside of it? Is being Roman the same in Rome and in Alexandria in Egypt in first century AD? Does the term Asian do justice to diverse ethnic and religious groups in Asia? In Section 1 of this Element, I explained how problematic the term ancient Egyptians is because it groups people of different age, gender, class, etc., not respecting their diverse experiences. Equally, there is no reason we should consider Egyptian neighbours to have been less diverse on these and other aspects of identity.

P. W. Stockhammer has effectively argued that archaeologists perceive those objects as hybrids which seem to resist classification within predetermined taxonomies (Stockhammer, 2013: 11–13). The fact that some authors tend to explore cultural mixture by taking the hybrid apart and seek out its source components (Van Valkenburgh, 2013: 305) indicates that this has little to do with postcolonial notion of hybridity.

For example, in ancient Egyptian art, there are cases of hybrid foreign figures which have iconographic elements of different groups combined; for example, Syrian-Aegean hybrid figures from the fifteenth century BC tombs of Puimre (Figure 9) and Menkheperreseneb, both high officials of their time. P. Rehak, an archaeologist specialising in the Bronze Age Aegean, argued that these hybrid figures maybe represent a mixture of the two or more populations which can be

Figure 9 Aegean-Syrian hybrid figure, third from the left, among rulers from the North, 'Asia', from the tomb of Puimre
(after Davies, 1922: Pl. I)

expected 'in some of the cosmopolitan port towns of Syria-Palestine or the Nile Delta in the Late Bronze Age' (Rehak, 1998: 47). Some Egyptologists argued that these iconographic hybrid figures could derive from accurate observations of the crews of the trading vessels docked in the Egyptian ports. It has been suggested that the men of the Uluburun ship, a fourteenth century BC shipwreck in south-western Turkey with material culture of diverse provenance, might have resembled these hybrids (Darnell & Manassa, 2007: 202).

Such interpretations tell us that these authors understood iconographic hybridism as a method of representing cultural mixture and that they understand cultural mixture as merging of two or more cultures. However, there have never existed 'down to the waist Aegeans and up to the waist Syrians', which does not mean that we should not take the hybrid figures into account at all. That these individuals actually did not look like this, does not mean that the crews of the trading ships did not have identities which are beyond the dichotomies we establish where ethnicity is concerned (e.g. Aegean, Syrian, or any other). Where Egyptian iconography is concerned, these hybrid figures have to be understood through principles of representation and decorum in which like is hybridised with like. There are no hybrid figures combining northern and southern Egyptian neighbours. During the fifteenth century BC and later, both Aegeans and Syrians are associated with the north in Egyptian cultural geography (Quack, 1996: 77–9; Safronov, 2017: 750–3) and therefore it should come as no surprise that figures from these regions could be hybridised (Matić, 2014b: 282–7).

Precisely because archaeologists more often than not confuse visual hybridism with the postcolonial concept of hybridism, some alternatives have been proposed. Ph. Stockhammer prefers the term entanglement to hybridity, hybridism, and hybridisation for several reasons. He argues that in postcolonial studies these terms are used as political metaphor and also that they have pejorative biological background (Stockhammer, 2012: 89). For him, entanglement is a concept to be used to describe the phenomena that are the result of the creative process triggered by intercultural encounters (Stockhammer, 2013: 16). He distinguishes between material and relational entanglement where the first refers to an entangled object and the second to entanglement of past practices with an object (Stockhammer, 2013: 23). The term entanglement has also found its way into the archaeology of Egypt and Nubia. For example, K. Liszka uses it for previously mentioned dry-stone architecture at mining sites in the Eastern desert. She argues that the case of architecture in Egyptian design but Nubian building tradition represents 'entangled cultures; the forms of one culture are created with the material technique of another' (Liszka, 2017: 14). There are numerous other authors who utilise the term nowadays and there is not enough space here to refer to all of them. A close read of recent works actually shows that rather than utilising the concept and what it epistemologically refers to, many authors frequently simply use the word.

Another case is often discussed by those Egyptologists close to postcolonial theory and the concept of the hybrid. This is the case of Hekanefer, prince of Miam, during the time of Egyptian control of Nubia from fifteenth to eleventh century BC. Hekanefer was administrator of ancient Miam (Aniba in Lower Nubia) and answered to Huy, viceroy of Nubia during the reign of Tutankhamun in the fourteenth century BC. In the tomb of Huy in Thebes, Hekanefer is depicted as a Nubian in a tribute scene together with other Nubians (Figure 10), but in his own tomb in Nubia (Figure 11) he is depicted as an Egyptian official. In fact, his tomb is a tomb of an Egyptian official, as both its decoration and equipment match those of the Egyptian elite from Egypt. Egyptologists interpret the case of Hekanefer in different ways. There are those who argue that Hekanefer was required to appear as a Nubian at the Egyptian court, because the entire context of his appearance there, namely a New Year's festival, was a showcase of royal ideology (Smith, 2007: 240), or because he was simply still seen as Nubian by Egyptians (Kemp, 2018: 38). Others suggested that Hekanefer had a specific double identity (van Pelt, 2013). What we have to bear in mind is that we are comparing two entirely different forms of evidence.

In the tomb of Huy, Hekanefer and other Nubians are depicted in a tribute scene – a term used by Egyptologists to describe visual representation of an event which supposedly occurred once a year in Egypt during the celebration of the New Year. During the event, foreign emissaries of different status vis-à-vis Egypt and each other would bring various objects, resources, and people to the Egyptian king. These scenes existed at least from the time of Hatshepsut in fifteenth century BC and by the time of Tutankhamun they were well established and structured (Hallmann, 2006). There were certain rules on how to depict whom, which does not mean that the artists could not deviate from these rules in different contexts. In the tribute scene from the tomb of Huy, Hekanefer is not depicted by himself. In the case of his own tomb he would have had more agency where decoration and his self-representation was concerned, as construction of his tomb started when he was still living. The comparison would be on a different epistemological level if we were comparing two different representations initiated by Hekanefer himself. This is not the case here. It is even questionable if he actually appeared at the Egyptian court the way he is depicted in the tomb of Huy. Only if we could be sure this was the case, could we then discuss his agency behind this type of appearance. The artists who painted the tribute scene from the tomb of Huy worked with an already existing pattern and were not necessarily present at the ceremony in which Hekanefer and his

Figure 10 Hekanefer as a Nubian ruler in the tribute scene from the tomb of Huy, viceroy of Nubia under Tutankhamun (https://www.metmuseum.org/art/collection/search/548571)

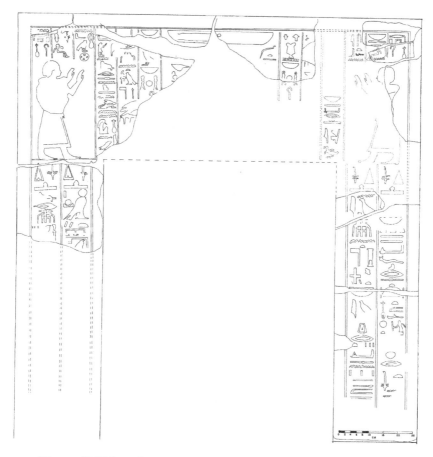

Figure 11 Hekanefer as an Egyptian in his tomb in Toshka, Nubia
(redrawn after Simpson, 1963: fig. 7)

entourage appeared. The fact that they depicted them as Nubians wearing both Nubian and Egyptian dress indicates that the artists creatively adjusted the established pattern to a new situation. If they had depicted Hekanefer and his entourage entirely as Egyptian officials, the purpose of the tribute scene to present an ecumenic dominion of the pharaoh over foreign lands would have been lost.

Whether or not the case of Hekanefer is a case of hybridity, understood as in the work of H. Bhabha, is a complicated question. This is primarily because we lack evidence that Hekanefer, as a man of Nubian origin in Egyptian state apparatus, used his position to question the authority of Egyptian state or culture. A recent suggestion that 'tribute scenes such as the one at TT40, depicting Nubians bringing gold and other treasures from their country, could have been interpreted by Nubians as expression of their own power and their ability to provide Egypt with resources' (Lemos, 2020: 7) is not supported by evidence. The event tribute scenes depicted were pharaoh centred, as indicated by numerous diplomatic letters in which the rulers of foreign countries complain on how both the gifts and the emissaries they sent were misrepresented or mistreated during such an event (Matić, 2017; Matić, 2019). We should equally not consider Hekanefer and his entourage to have been naïve on their position in the state apparatus. The state of Egypt exploited Nubian resources and although some of the locals have rebelled, others were cooperating with Egyptians. The worst mistake pseudo postcolonial revisions can make is to generalise the 'colonisers' into nonviolent and friendly settlers, and the 'subaltern' into naïve people devoid of motives and strategies.

Rather, on the contrary, Hekanefer's burial in Nubia indicates that he used his position in Egyptian state apparatus to his own benefits, profiling himself within a diaspora Lower Nubian community of Egyptians and Nubians as a member of the Egyptian elite. It is indeed tempting to see this as related to ethnic identity, however, Hekanefer does not present himself as just any Egyptian. Status plays the most significant role here.

3.5.2 Mimicry

Mimicry, in the work of H. Bhabha, is almost like an imitation, but not quite the same, as exact imitation would not have the main aspect of mimicry, and that is the potential to question the normative systems of knowledge, the colonial discourse, and relations of power (Bhabha, 1994: 91–120). We have an example for this social phenomenon attested in the Amarna letters. These are diplomatic letters written in the Akkadian language, lingua franca of the Late Bronze Age Near East and found in Tell el-Amarna, capital of Egypt during the reign of Akhenaten in fourteenth century BC. In one of these letters (EA 4), the king of Babylon asks for any Egyptian woman to be sent to him in marriage. He adds that no one in Babylon will know that she is not a princess. Clearly, the king of Babylon is insisting on one thing only and that is that the woman sent by the pharaoh is an Egyptian woman. Several scholars have already noted that the king of Egypt, just as other Late Bronze Age kings, gladly took foreign women, often daughters of foreign kings, for wives. However, there are indications that he did not send Egyptian women to be married to foreign kings as gladly. By having an Egyptian woman represented at his court as an Egyptian princess, the king of Babylon attempted to achieve a mimic effect that would elevate his status (Matić, 2017: 100).

This example demonstrates that mimicry can be used to question Egyptian authority; however, here this is not done by mimicking ethnic identity, rather, the ethnic identity of the requested woman is seen as a possibility for expression of an elevated status of the Babylonian king. Unlike in the case of Hekanefer, the status of this woman plays no role here, at least not for the king of Babylon.

3.5.3 Third Space

Other concepts frequent in postcolonial theory have found their way into the archaeology of Egypt too. B. Bader calls the diverse community at Tell el-Dabᶜa creole (Bader, 2011: 62). L. Steel argues that second-millennium BC Gaza of the southern Levant was a cosmopolitan period characterised by Egyptian colonial activity. Accordingly, the communities at either end of the Way of Horus, an ancient road leading from Egypt to Levant, both in the Nile Delta and around the mouth of Gaza, were creolised (Steel, 2018: 24). As an example, she gives the use of Egyptian-style anthropomorphic clay coffins, which she argues were used by Egyptianised locals who appropriated only some aspects of Egyptian funerary customs, whereas other customs one would expect if the deceased were Egyptian (e.g. mummification) were not present (Steel, 2018: 22).

However, the term creole has a specific historical background: it originally refers to ethnic groups originating in colonial era of the sixteenth to nineteenth century, after the mixing of European colonisers and people from the colonies. This phenomenon is different than emergence of creole languages which are developed from simplifying and mixing of different languages into a new one. The difference between creole phenomena of the colonial era and the phenomena of third and second millennium BC in Egypt is the scale of the encounter. Unlike in the colonial era, when Europeans and some people from the colonies encountered each other for the first time, ancient Egyptians had long history of contact with their neighbours. The effects of such encounters simply cannot be the same.

These examples serve to demonstrate that reflexivity towards terms we use and theories we apply should not remain only as points of criticism towards early authors, but also as a constant reminder to ourselves not to overlook historical contingency of the concepts we ourselves use. More specific discussions on ethnicity found in the vast field of postcolonial studies are rarely consulted. According to L. Hutcheon, 'any sense of ethnicity is bound to be configured differently in a new place because of the inevitable changes that come with displacement' (Hutcheon et al., 1998: 30). We must bear in mind that people can find themselves in unhomely situations. Unhomely is another term related to H. Bhabha who describes it as capturing 'something of the estranging sense of the relocation of the home and the world in an unhallowed place' (Bhabha, 1992: 141). For example, Toronto's 1990s Little Italy lacked a cultural resemblance to the Italy of the same time. What we learn from historical archaeologists investigating colonialism is that changes can occur in a society to such a level that they can limit the use of simple analogies between the society in question and its diaspora, one example for this being African societies and their American diasporas (Cruz, 2011: 338). This is a warning to Egyptologists when they compare the archaeological record of ancient Egyptian core and their presence in, for example, the lands Egyptians conquered and controlled such as Nubia and Syria-Palestine. Neither the 'core' nor the 'periphery' were homogenous. H. Bhabha uses the term third space as a metaphor to describe the negotiation of differences between cultures. This negotiation produces tension specific for borderline existences (Bhabha, 1992: 218). However, the term third space is often confused by archaeologists for actual space of encounter. Rather, it is a metaphor for a specific kind of encounter with unforeseen consequences on all who took part in it (Matić, 2017: 103–4). Thus, instead of approaching ancient Egyptian encounters with foreigners as if we already knew their results, we should open the possibilities to the unplanned, unexpected, and different consequences these encounters could have had for all sides.

3.6 Intersectionality

Identity is multiscalar (Voss, 2008: 13), meaning that people rarely have the same experiences as others. Being a man or a woman, young or old, or members of an ethnic group can result in vastly different experiences. Additional differences come into play where class or status is concerned, and in some societies even sexuality and other aspects of identity also come into play. Therefore, intersectionality is a concept which reminds us that ethnic identity cannot be looked for or studied in isolation from other forms of identity. For example, to be a proper Nafana in Ghana is to be born of a Nafana woman who went through Nafana nobility and marriage rites, including circumcision (Cruz, 2011: 344).

Intersectionality is a concept rarely considered by Egyptologists, although there are some notable exceptions (e.g. Meskell, 1999, although she does not deal with ethnic identity; Moers 2016: 694). For example, K. Liszka discusses the case of a woman named Aashyet, from twenty-first century BC Egypt, who on her sarcophagus is, together with some other female members of her household, depicted with dark skin. Liszka argues that we have to bear in mind her gender, occupation (priestess of goddess Hathor), and status in order to understand her choosing to be depicted with dark skin instead of yellowish skin according to gender convention for women in ancient Egypt (Liszka, 2018).

Clearly there was also a gender background of different status for the Nubians depicted in the tribute scene from the tomb of Huy from the reign of Tutankhamun (Figure 10) and age-related gender differences among Nubian women depicted in the tribute scene from the tomb of Rekhmire (TT 100) from the reign of Thutmose III in fifteenth century BC (Figure 12). Different groups of Nubian women depicted here, namely those with children, those without children, and those depicted as young girls, correspond to different categories Egyptians used for captured women in their lists of spoils of war, namely married/with child, social virgin/not married, and young girl. Such a division does not necessarily correspond to age/gender categories among the Nubians, nevertheless it is imposed by the Egyptian administration (Matić, 2020).

Whereas some Nubian women from the scene from the tomb of Huy can be interpreted as being part of Hekanefer's high-status elite household, with perhaps his wife and daughters among them, other women from this tribute scene are Nubian prisoners accompanied by their children (Pemler, 2018). There has also been a suggestion that the representation of an elite Nubian woman dressed as an Egyptian woman and riding in a chariot pulled by cattle was meant to be mocked by the viewers of the scene in the tomb of Huy (Burmeister, 2013: 138). Still, others have challenged this, because apart from the unique combination of a 'princess' and chariot pulled by oxen there is nothing else to indicate mockery. D. Pemler suggests that oxen are depicted instead of horses because Nubians of this period were more famous for their cattle (Pemler, 2018: 37).

These cases are just some of many which warn us that experiences of ethnic identity were different depending on age, gender, and status, at least, and there must have been other factors involved as well.

4 Third Science Revolution

4.1 Archaeology and the Third Science Revolution

The old idea that identity may be read from the bones of ancient peoples (Section 2) is slowly reviving in archaeology. Advances in analyses of ancient DNA and stable isotopes have triggered considerable new research. The DNA data can be used to identify statistical groupings of individuals who share more genetic variants with each other than with individuals outside these groups (Eisenmann et al., 2018). Isotopes of strontium, oxygen, and lead have been used in the studies of provenance of human remains. Analyses involve comparison of isotope ratios in tooth enamel and bone. As the enamel in teeth forms in early childhood and undergoes little change, it is a reliable indicator of strontium isotopes. Human bone is more dynamic. Values in human teeth indicating place of birth and early

Figure 12 Nubian women of different age in the tribute scene from the tomb of Rekhmire (TT 100), vizier of Thutmose III (redrawn after Davies, 1943: Pls. XXI and XXII, graphic A. Hassler, ÖAI/ÖAW)

childhood which do not match those from bone (place of death) indicate immi-grants (Weiner, 2010: 32–5). These developments in science and their implications in archaeology have been quite optimistically termed 'the third science revolution' (Kristiansen, 2014).

This optimism did not go without criticism aimed at the assumption that 'the third science revolution' would cause much necessary critical discussions on ethnicity. Critical thinking involves examining the premises and frames even before the data is collected and analysed, or more precisely even before the data is produced (Niklasson, 2014: 59). For example, whereas, so-called hard sci-ence identifies Phoenician DNA, historians are uncomfortable with even speak-ing about Phoenicians (McInerney, 2014: 5). Although analyses might be state of the art, the way the data is sampled and the samples are interpreted is often anything but. For example, teeth of specific individuals are used to provide samples for analyses, however, these individuals are chosen to be representa-tives of different prehistoric archaeological cultures which still match the ones mapped by V. G. Childe (Hakenbeck, 2019). Thus, genetic samples stand not only for teeth of different individuals, they stand for entire archaeological cultures which are in this process understood as ethnic groups (see Section 2 for details). The same logic of culture-historical archaeology is now applied not on pots representing people, but on physical remains representing 'peoples'. In some cases, individuals were found with genetic make-up significantly different than the rest of the population of the cemetery in which they were buried, although all could be classified as belonging to a single archaeological culture (Eisenmann et al., 2018). An additional problem with most of the attempts to correlate cultural and genetic evidence is the assumption of endogamy as the norm throughout history and across cultures (Chrisomalis & Trigger, 2003: 5). Marrying only within the limits of a local community cannot be assumed before the analyses are done.

Although DNA and isotope analyses can help us to identify individuals whose genetic makeup differs from the rest of the community, indicating that they are either foreigners or descendants of foreigners, these analyses are not enough for studies of ethnic identity.

4.2 Egyptology and Third Science Revolution

This new hype has also found its way into the archaeology of Egypt, and, not surprisingly, with this came the associated problematic assumptions on ethnic identity that are rooted in culture-historical archaeology. For example, it has been suggested that DNA analysis could provide the answer to the question of Maiherperi's ethnic identity (Lakomy, 2016: 308). Maiherperi was the child of the royal nursery and fanbearer on the king, probably under king Thutmose III in fifteenth century BC, and was buried in the Valley of the Kings (KV 36), which was a rare privilege. In vignettes of his *Book of the Dead* papyrus (CG 24095), Maiherperi is depicted with dark brown skin colour and in one case with curly hair reaching his chin (Lakomy, 2016: Tf. 135, Abb. 530, Tf. 148, Abb. 556). This is usually interpreted as a Nubian feature, also argued to be confirmed by his mummy (Schneider, 2010: 115; Smith, 2007: 230). Therefore, Egyptologists tend to interpret Maiherperi as an assimilated Nubian. The idea that his 'real' identity can be uncovered using ancient DNA demonstrates a primordial understanding of ethnic identity (see Section 3 for details). The actual social practices of Maiherperi are silently considered less important than the depiction of his skin.

There are numerous problems with the idea that isotopes and DNA can solve the enigmas of ethnic identities. One of these problems is strictly methodological. The Nile's complex fluvial regime, together with the underlying geology of the Nile Valley and Nile's source regions, pose problems for isotope analyses (Woodward et al., 2015). Another problem is the pristine preservation of collagen in some contexts, such are the sites in the Sudan because of the heat and dry sandy soil (Spencer, Stevens & Binder, 2017: 46). Geological research has pointed to the impact of aeolian sands on the sedimentary composition of the Nile and its tributaries as a major confounding factor in the strontium signatures of water. Being that these are highly variable, and depend on climatic conditions, they could significantly alter isotopic values and potentially lead to erroneous conclusions (Binder, 2019: 114; Woodward et al., 2015). M. R. Buzon and her associates claim that it was possible to identify individuals from Thebes in Upper Egypt at the Nubian site of Tombos in Upper Nubia because strontium at Tombos probably comes from soil rather than the Nile water (Buzon, Simonetti & Creaser, 2007: 1400). In another study of strontium isotope values from the Tombos cemetery sample, M. R. Buzon and A. Simonetti argue that during the period from *c.*1550–1070 BC, individuals from Egypt can be traced at the site and that during first millennium BC only locals can be traced, with some immigrants possibly coming from the south (Buzon & Simonetti, 2013: 7). However, the recent study of Nile's fluvial regimes and its influence on isotope analyses stressed that caution is necessary in interpreting the results in such manner (Woodward et al., 2015). The most recent study of strontium isotope ratios of samples from nine individuals from tomb 26 from cemetery SAC 5 on Sai island in Upper Nubia argues that all of them were local. The burial, itself dating to fifteenth to thirteenth century BC, was found as part of an Egyptian-style rock-hewn shaft tomb with a pyramid as a superstructure. It contained two painted wooden coffins, scarabs, faience vessels, pottery vessels, and one stone shabti figurine, fragments of funerary masks with inlayed eyes and gold foil. According to the inscribed finds, the burial belonged to Khnumose who was an Overseer of Goldsmiths and his unnamed wife (Retzmann et al., 2019). These individuals had an Egyptian burial with Egyptian material culture. Khnumose had an Egyptian name and an Egyptian title. Clearly, his Nubian origin, as in the cases of Hekanefer (Section 3) and Maiherperi, was not an obstacle in having a prestigious occupation under Egyptian rule and being member of the Egyptian elite.

A study of ancient Egyptian mummy genomes published by V. J. Schuenemann and her associates, aimed to investigate changes and continuities in the genetic makeup of the inhabitants of the Abusir el-Meleq in region of the Fayum in antiquity. One statement in this paper particularly deserves critical attention: 'Particularly, in the first millennium BCE Egypt endured foreign domination leading to growing numbers of foreigners living within its borders possibly contributing genetically to the local population' (Schuenemann et al., 2017: 1).

Several phenomena are confused here. Foreign rule (dominations) is understood as a factor leading to a growing number of foreigners. The first millennium BC division of the previously united land led to the emergence of the Libyan Dynasty in the north, and later to the conquering of Egypt by Kushite kings from Nubia. However, these Libyan kings used Egyptian iconography and language, prayed to Egyptian gods, and were buried as Egyptian kings (Vittmann, 2003). The population from which they came had been living in Egypt for centuries until men bearing names of Libyan origin took over power in one part of the land. It all comes down to understanding these individuals as foreigners because of the non-Egyptian origin of their personal names. As we have seen in the previous section, this is a very problematic assumption. The same can be said for the Kushite rulers of Egypt during *c.*750–650 BC. Although bringing with them some inherently Kushite elements of royal ideology, kingship, religion, and kinship they still also used Egyptian iconography and language, prayed to Egyptian gods, and were buried in a tradition with predominately Egyptian elements. The same may be said for the private personas of Kushite descent buried in Egypt. There is no comprehensive evidence based on textual sources and archaeology that an increased number of people of various origins came to Egypt in the first half of the first millennium BC (Budka, 2019). This increase in foreign presence because of foreign rule is even less evident during the Assyrian (seventh century BC) and Persian (sixth to fourth century BC) rule of Egypt (Vittmann, 2003). It seems that the first real demographic changes began slowly after Persian rule and especially during Ptolemaic and Roman rule of Egypt, from fourth century BC onwards (Riggs, 2005; Rowlandson, 2013).

The study of Schuenemann and her associates was based on ninety mitochondrial genomes and genome-wide data sets from three individuals from Abusir el-Meleq in Middle Egypt and dating from the sixteenth century BC to the Roman period (30 BC to seventh century AD). Some 166 samples were taken from 151 mummified individuals. They group the individuals according to radiocarbon dates into three groups: pre-Ptolemaic (from *c.*1550–300 BC), Ptolemaic (from *c.*300 to 31 BC) and Roman (30 BC to seventh century AD). This is problematic if one bears in mind that the individuals from the first group come from a time span of almost 1,250 years, the second group of almost 300 years, and the third group of almost 700 years. There are also some statements which are given rather uncritically. Namely, the authors assume that there was a large-scale immigration of Canaanite population which they describe as 'known as the Hyksos' into Lower Egypt during the second millennium BC. This is surprising because the argument of Canaanite invasion is based on the culture-historical 'pots equal people' assumption which is criticised by Schuenemann and her associates at the beginning of the paper. The Hyksos are, as we have seen in Section 2, originally a reference to the ruling class of Avaris and not its entire population, which consisted of people of local and foreign origin and new migrants from the eastern Mediterranean. It is erroneous to treat the population of Avaris as a closed population in an anthropological sense which can then be compared to other populations, for example, those in the Levant (Forstner-Müller & Müller, 2006: 96). Striking similarities can be noticed between the studies on ancient DNA of prehistoric Europe and the studies of DNA of ancient Egypt. A critical reflection towards both terms used and methods applied is necessary.

Another similar study aims to use DNA and isotope analyses to solve the problem of the origin of the population of Avaris during the first half of the second millennium BC. 'The Hyksos Enigma' project of M. Bietak, as principal investigator, and his associates aims to 'reveal the origin of the western Asiatic population' of the Eastern Delta (https://thehyksosenigma .oeaw.ac.at/about/, 05.08.2019). It seems that large-scale immigration is assumed even before the analysis is conducted. In fact, in one interview published on 5 February 2016, M. Bietak stated: 'Certain events repeat themselves. Ancient history also knew massive flows of migration, and this is something we are seeing today. I assume that 50 years from now a considerable share of the European population will have oriental roots. Perhaps one can hope that people will become acculturated and contribute to a successful Europe of the future' (https://scilog.fwf.ac.at/en, 05.08.2019). In Section 2, we have seen that most of such assumptions are based on culture-historical methodology.

Within this project, H. Schutkowski and his team work on skeletal remains from the site and on stable isotope and ancient DNA analyses. At a conference of the

American Association of Physical Anthropologists in March 2019, N. Maaranen, S. R. Zakrzewski and H. Schutkowski (2019) presented the results of their study of dental material of ninety-six individuals from three areas of Tell el-Dabᶜa. The results were compared with ancient Egyptian cemeteries at Lisht (*c.*2000–1800 BC), Thebes (*c.*2130–1800 BC), and Qurna (*c.*1300–1190 BC). According to the results of this study, the material from Tell el-Dabᶜa is distant from the material from Lisht, Thebes, and Qurna, 6–14 times more than standard deviation. They refer to the material from Tell el-Dabᶜa as Hyksos and argue that, based on these results, they were not of Egyptian origin. However, none of the burials from Tell el-Dabᶜa is a royal burial, so the use of the term Hyksos is not justified: it is clear that it is used here as an ethnic designation for the entire population of Avaris. Furthermore, the results of this study show some difference between the material from Lisht, Qurna, and Thebes. In fact, the difference between Lisht and Thebes is greater than the difference between Qurna and Thebes. This is not surprising considering the geographical distribution of these sites (Figure 1) and the chronological range of the samples. Dental material differs greatly from Avaris on one side and Lisht, Qurna, and Thebes on the other, but one should consider a wide range of possibilities for such differences, including, among others, different life conditions in the Delta, and the fact that it is closer to the Levant. Its population must have been different than that of the south throughout much of ancient Egyptian history (Kemp, 2018: 50), but to what extent it can be said that it was not Egyptian is a matter which cannot be answered using such methods.

The most recent study of strontium isotopes ratios from human tooth enamel was conducted on seventy-five individuals from three different cemeteries at Tell el-Dabᶜa, out of which thirty-six were from pre-Hyksos rule and thirty-five from Hyksos rule contexts. The results showed that more than half spent their lives outside of the Nile Delta, displaying a wide range of values and more 'immigrants' in the pre-Hyksos period, with more women non-locals than men. However, it was not possible to exactly pinpoint the origin of the non-locals (Stantis et al., 2020). Still, we have to bear in mind that a study of seventy-five individuals out of which sixty-seven come from area A/II, seven from area F/I, and one from area A/I, can hardly be representative of the entire population of the site of some 260 ha and some 1,000 tombs excavated until now. An additional problem is that, although at the beginning of the paper Stantis et al. stress that they will use the term Hyksos to refer to the ruling class only, at the end of the paper, based on the results of the study, they state that 'in combination with previous archaeological evidence, this research supports the concept that the Hyksos were not an invading force occupying this city and the upper Nile Delta, but an internal group of people who gained power in a system with which they were already familiar' (Stantis et al., 2020: 9). Again, we have the equation of the Hyksos with the 'people' inhabiting the site, now referring to the non-local women whose exact origin could actually not be pinpointed.

5 Concluding Remarks

The question of identity, whether racial in the nineteenth and early twentieth century or ethnic in the later twentieth and twenty-first century, continues to occupy Egyptologists. Contemporary Egyptology faces the same problems in studying ethnic identity in the past as other historical disciplines, no matter if they are based on texts, images, material culture, or their various combinations. Even those who did not or do not deal with these questions, classify, for example, the archaeological material such as pottery (into e.g. Egyptian and Nubian) and use it as evidence of actual foreign presence. It is rarely considered that although foreigners could have been there, the foreign material culture can be used by locals too, without them necessarily aspiring to foreign identity. Section 3 demonstrated the difficulties which go together with such arguments.

Ancient Egypt presents us with an excellent case for studying ethnogenesis as defined in Section 3, a concept unfortunately rarely used by Egyptologists. Following S. Jones, ethnic identities are based on shifting, situational, subjective identifications of self and others, rooted in daily practices and historical experiences, and subject to transformations and discontinuity (Jones, 1997: 13). Numerous examples discussed in this Element demonstrate this. Identity in ancient Egypt was not as fixed as primordialists would argue. The old Egyptological idea of a single Egyptian culture with single common ethnic identity, language, and shared values cannot be accounted for in all contexts (Baines, 1996: 362; contra Kemp, 2018: 24–5, who lists these elements in defining ancient Egyptians as a nation). A person of foreign descent could become Egyptian no matter his or her background. This has led some authors to argue that 'foreignness' loses its applicability in the setting in which people of foreign origin who lived in Egypt adapted to the social and cultural system of their host country (Schneider, 2010: 144; also Budka, 2012).

The long history of ancient Egypt and the various examples provided in this Element teach us that an essentialist notion of ethnic identity simply does not hold ground. What it meant to be Egyptian or a foreigner changed significantly and numerous times over at least three millennia. It was negotiated and defined in contrast not to diverse people of foreign origin who lived in Egypt and spoke Egyptian, for example, but to people who lived outside of Egypt, not speaking the Egyptian language, and even possibly sometimes threatening the land of Egypt. This is why both the scientific racism discussed in Section 2 and the third science revolution and its tools such as DNA and isotope analyses discussed in Section 4, fail to give answers to ethnic identity being that it is socially constructed (Lucy, 2005: 93). We have to differentiate between biological proximity-divergence and ethnic identity, as the former is 'a result of long history of interactions that occur between that person's ancestors and earlier natural and sociocultural environments' (Buzon, 2008: 166). Although 'groups with similar cranial shape tend to be related more closely to each other than groups that show more divergence' (Buzon, 2008: 166), these similarities and differences are not ethnic *differentia specifica*. Feeling as a member of and identifying with an ethnic groups is not something written in bone, blood, or DNA. These analyses are certainly more than useful in studying ethnicity because they provide us with valuable information on origin, descent, biological kinship, and mobility. But as texts and iconography teach us, foreignness read through these analyses can mean little, because it was not an obstacle to self-identification or outside recognition of membership to a certain ethnic group. Studying cultures which left rich textual and visual record behind, such as ancient Egypt, provides a nice balance to the approaches relying solely on skeletal remains of ancient people, like in the case of prehistory.

The stereotypical, rhetorical, and ideological representations of foreigners in texts and iconography are a reference to the process of self-definition and do not target the inhabitants of Egypt of different descent, as long as they are loyal to the king. Cultural practices of foreign origin can be used to express status rather than ethnic identity and can as such slowly but surely inspire others to adopt them (Schneider, 2003). After some time, they become an integral part of one's own unconscious daily (habitus) or occasional practices, losing the allure of foreignness. This is why foreign material culture and practices documented in the archaeological record cannot be interpreted in a culture-historical manner as evidence of foreign presence using the pots equals people premise. This does not mean that people do not move and leave archaeological traces of their movement or presence. Some of these movements leave archaeological traces, others do not. Yet, recognising a foreign burial in ancient Egypt does not mean studying ethnic identity. We should always remember that the dead are buried by the community of the living, so that those who might have tried to change their ways still got buried in the way the community they once belonged to wanted them to be buried. This was probably one of the reasons textual sources indicate that ancient Egyptians preferred being buried at home (Section 1).

One should, however, not be pessimistic and depart from any attempt at studying ethnic identity through material culture. In fact, material culture is crucial for expressing ethnic identity. None of the afore-mentioned people of foreign origin could express either their foreignness, or their Egyptianness without material culture (e.g. dress, funerary stelae, tombs). However, what culture-historical archaeology fails to recognise is that not all material culture is used by a group or recognised by another group as an ethnic marker. What we use to group ourselves or differentiate ourselves from the others can be used by others to mark us, but they can also mark us with that which we do not recognise as a differentiating feature. Pottery and culinary practices can be adopted or abandoned. People can also try things out, sometimes out of curiosity, continue to use them, or abandon them completely. But that does not mean that foreigners were not around; they could have been, sometimes longer, sometimes occasionally.

Egyptology benefits a lot from rich textual and iconographic sources. The danger is, however, in insufficient dialogue between Egyptologists specialising in philology and historiography, and those specialising in archaeology and art history. Even more dangerous is the lack of awareness of discussions on ethnicity outside of Egyptology, namely in the broader archaeological world and other disciplines, such as sociology and anthropology. Egyptologists rarely stressed that 'what we must do is try to avoid applying inappropriate modern distinctions to the ancient situation' (Johnson, 1999: 211). In Section 1, we have seen that ancient Egyptian identity was never 'national', although in certain periods there is evidence of 'imperial identity' of the elitist segment of Egyptian society (Moers 2016, 701). The need to rethink our preconceived notions of identity, the concepts we employ to interpret the past, and the way we understand material culture is gaining increased recognition. T. Schneider labelled these efforts 'trans-Egyptology of 21st century' (Schneider, 2018: 246). However, while preliminary moves have been made in the last two decades or so, at least where the topic covered by this Element is concerned, still only a handful of scholars participate in these discussions. Most Egyptologists are instead what some archaeologists call 'culture happy', meaning that they still work within the frame of culture-historical archaeology (see Section 2). Instead, starting from the notion of Egyptian identity being very locally bound, we should ask ourselves in which context this locally bound identity can be elevated to sentiments of belonging to a land or a people. It seems that this is in the case of supra-local and supra-regional mobility (Moers, 2016: 699) or tensions (Sections 1 and Section 3).

This Element has made an attempt to fill gaps in communication between studies of ethnic identity both inside and outside Egyptology, and those not dealing with these questions, by providing an overview of both past and current approaches, problems, and challenges Egyptologists face in studying ethnicity. Readers still interested in this topic should further venture into the rich world of

Egyptological studies of foreigners and ethnicity, and the even richer world of numerous and varied ancient Egyptian sources. The sources (textual, iconographic, and archaeological) can be surely read and studied to learn more than has been said here and, if this is the outcome, my goal with this Element is accomplished.

References

Allen, J. P. (2015). *Middle Egyptian Literature: Eight Literary Works of the Middle Kingdom*. Cambridge: Cambridge University Press.

Anthony, F. B. (2016). *Foreigners in Ancient Egypt: Theban Tomb Paintings from the Early Eighteenth Dynasty (1550–1372 BC)*. London: Bloomsbury.

Arnold, D. (2010). Image and Identity: Egypt's Eastern Neighbours, East Delta People and the Hyksos. In M. Marée, ed., *The Second Intermediate Period (13th–I 7th Dynasties): Current Research, Future Prospects*. Orientalia Lovaniensia Analecta 192. Leuven: Peeters, pp. 183–221.

Assmann, J. (1996). Zum Konzept der Fremdheit im alten Ägypten. In M. Schuster, ed., *Die Begegnung mit dem Fremden: Wertungen und Wirkungen in Hochkulturen vom Altertum bis zur Gegenwart*. Colloquium Rauricum 4. Stuttgart & Leipzig: Teubner, pp. 77–99.

Bader, B. (2011). Contacts between Egypt and Syria-Palestine as Seen in a Grown Settlement of the Late Middle Kingdom at Tell el-Dabᶜa/Egypt. In J. Mynářová, ed., *Egypt and the Near East: The Crossroads, Proceedings of the International Workshop on the Relations between Egypt and the Near East in the Bronze Age, Prague 2011*. Prague: Charles University, pp. 41–72.

Bader, B. (2013). Cultural Mixing in Egyptian Archaeology: The 'Hyksos' as a Case Study. In W. P. van Pelt, ed., *Archaeology and Cultural Mixing*. Archaeological Review from Cambridge Issue 28.1. Cambridge: Archaeological Review Cambridge, pp. 257–86.

Baines, J. (1996). Contextualising Egyptian Representations of Society and Ethnicity. In J. Cooper & G. Schwartz, eds., *The Study of the Ancient Near East in Twenty-First Century*. Winona Lake: Eisenbrauns, pp. 339–84.

Barth, F. (1969). *Ethnic Groups and Boundaries*. Boston: Little, Brown.

Becker, M. (2016). Female Influence, aside from that of the God's Wives of Amun, during the Third Intermediate Period. In M. Becker, A. I. Blöbaum & A. Lohwasser, eds., *'Prayer and Power': Proceedings of the Conference on the God's Wives of Amun in Egypt during the First Millennium BC*. Ägypten und Altes Testament 84. Münster: Ugarit Verlag, pp. 21–46.

Bentley, G. C. (1987). Ethnicity and Practice. *Comparative Studies in Society and History* **29**, 24–55.

Bestock, L. (2018). *Violence and Power in Ancient Egypt: Image and Ideology before the New Kingdom*. London & New York: Routledge.

Bhabha, H. (1992). The World and the Home. *Social Text* **31/32**, Third World and Post-Colonial Issues, 141–53,

Bhabha, H. (1994). *The Location of Culture*. London & New York: Routledge.

Bietak, M. (1966). *Ausgrabungen in Sayala-Nubien 1961–1965: Denkmäler der C-Gruppe und der Pan-Gräber-Kultur*. Denkschriften der philosophisch-historischen Klasse 92. Wien: Verlag des Österreichischen Archäologischen Institutes.

Bietak, M. (1996). *Avaris-The Capital of the Hyksos: Recent Excavations at Tell el-Dabᶜa*. London: The Trustees of British Museum.

Bietak, M. (2016). The Egyptian Community in Avaris during the Hyksos Period. *Ägypten und Levante* **XXVI**, 263–74.

Bietak, M. (2018). The Many Ethnicities of Avaris: Evidence from Northern Borderland of Egypt. In J. Budka and J. Auenmüller, eds., *From Microcosm to Macrocosm: Individual households and cities in Ancient Egypt and Nubia*. Leiden: Sidestone Press, pp. 73–92.

Bietak, M., Dorner, J., & Jánosi P. (2001) Ausgrabungen in dem Palastbezirk von Avaris. Vorbericht Tell el-Dabᶜa/ᶜEzbet Helmi 1993–2000. *Ägypten und Levante* **XXI**, 27–119.

Bietak, M., Forstner-Müller, I., & Mlinar, C. (2001). The Beginning of the Hyksos Period at Tell el-Dabᶜa: A Subtle Change in Material Culture. In P. M. Fischer, ed., *Contributions to the Archaeology and History of the Bronze and Iron Ages in the Eastern Mediterranean. Studies in honour of Paul Åström*. Wien: Österreichisches Archäologisches Institut, pp. 171–81.

Binder, M. (2019). The Role of Physical Anthropology in Nubian Archaeology. In D. Raue, ed., *Handbook of Ancient Nubia*. Vol. 1. Berlin: De Gruyter, pp. 103–27.

Bourdieu, P. (1990). *The Logic of Practice*. Trans. R. Nice. Stanford: Stanford University Press.

Brass, P. (1993). Elite competition and the Origins of Ethnic Nationalism In J. G. Berameni et al., eds., *Nationalism in Europe. Past and present*. Santiago de Compostela: University of Santiago de Compostela, pp. 111–26.

Breasted, J. H. (1935). *Ancient Times. A History of the Early World: An Introduction to the Study of Ancient History and the Career of Early Man*. Revised 2nd Edition. Boston: Ginn and Company.

Bresciani, E. (1997). Foreigners. In S. Donadoni, ed., *The Egyptians*. Chicago: University of Chicago Press, pp. 221–54.

Budka, J. (2012). Individuen, indigene Gruppe oder integrierter Teil der ägyptischen Gesellschaft? Zur soziologischen Aussagekraft materieller Hinterlassenschaften von Kuschiten im spätzeitlichen Ägypten. In G. Neunert, K. Gabler & A. Verbovsek, eds., *Sozialisationen: Individuum-Gruppe-Gesellschaft. Beiträge der ersten Münchner Arbeitskreises Junge Aegyptologie (MAJA 1)*. Göttinger Orientforschungen Ägypten 51. Wiesbaden: Harrassowitz Verlag, pp. 45–60.

Budka, J. (2019). Nubians in the 1st Millennium BC in Egypt. In D. Raue, ed., *Handbook of Ancient Nubia*. Vol. 2. Berlin: De Gruyter, pp. 697–712.

Burmeister, S. (2013). Die Sicherung der ethnischen Ordnung: Das Wandbild eines eigenartigen nubischen Streitwagens im Grab des Huy, Vizekönig von Kusch (Neues Reich). *Journal of Egyptian History* **6**, 131–51.

Buzon, M. R. (2006). Biological and Ethnic Identity in New Kingdom Nubia: A Case Study from Tombos. *Current Anthropology* **47**(4), 683–95.

Buzon, M. R. (2008). A Bioarchaeological Perspective on Egyptian Colonialism in Nubia during the New Kingdom. *The Journal of Egyptian Archaeology* **94**, 165–81.

Buzon, M. R., Simonetti, A., & Creaser, R. A. (2007). Migration in the Nile Valley during the New Kingdom Period: A Preliminary Strontium Isotope Study. *Journal of Archaeological Science* **34**, 1391–401.

Buzon, M. R., & Simonetti, A. (2013). Strontium isotope (87Sr/86Sr) variability in the Nile Valley: Identifying residential mobility during ancient Egyptian and Nubian sociopolitical changes in the New Kingdom and Napatan periods. *American Journal of Physical Anthropology* **151**(1), 1–9.

Candelora, D. (2018). Entangled in Orientalism: How the Hyksos Became a Race. *Journal of Egyptian History* **11**, 45–72.

Challis, D. (2013). *The Archaeology of Race: The Eugenic Ideas of Francis Galton and Flinders Petrie*. London: Bloomsbury.

Challis, D. (2016). Skull Triangles: Flinders Petrie, Race Theory and Biometrics. *Bulletin of the History of Archaeology* **26**(1.5), 1–8.

Chantrain, G. (2019). About Egyptianity and Foreignness in Egyptian Texts: A Context-Sensitive Lexical Study. In J. Mynářová, M. Kilani & S. Alivernini eds., *A Stranger in the House: the Crossroads III. Proceedings of an International Conference on Foreigners in Ancient Egzptian and Near Eastern Societies of the Bronze Age held in Prague, September 10–13, 2018*. Prague: Charles University, pp. 49–72.

Childe, V. G. (1929). *The Danube in Prehistory*. Oxford: Oxford University Press.

Chrisomalis, S., & Trigger, B. (2003). Reconstructing Prehistoric Ethnicity: Problems and Possibilities. In J. V. Wright & J-L. Pilon eds., *A Passion for the Past: Papers in Honour of James F. Pendergast*. Archaeological Survey of Canada Mercury Series Paper 164. Gatineau, QB: Canadian Museum of Civilization, pp. 1–21.

Cohen, S. (2015). Interpretative Uses and Abuses of the Beni Hasan Tomb Painting. *Journal of Near Eastern Studies* **74**(1), 19–38.

Cole, E. M. (2015). Foreign Influence in the Late New Kingdom and Third Intermediate Period. In M. Pinarello, J. Yoo, J. Lundock & C. Walsh, eds., *Current Research in Egyptology 2014. Proceedings of the Fifteenth Annual*

Symposium, University College London & King's College London 2014. Ancient Egypt in a Global World. Oxford: Oxbow Books, pp. 113–20.

Cooney, W. A. (2011). Egypt's Encounter with the West: Race, Culture and Identity. In J. Corbelli, D. Boatright & C. Malleson, eds., *Current Research in Egyptology 2009. Proceedings of the Tenth Annual Symposium University of Liverpool 2009.* Oxford: Oxbow Books, pp. 43–52.

Cooper, J. (2018). Kushites Expressing 'Egyptian' Kingship: Nubian Dynasties in Hieroglyphic Texts and a Phantom Kushite King. *Ägypten und Levante* **XXVIII**, 143–67.

Cornell, P. (2004). Social identity, the Body and Power. In F. Fahlander & T. Oestigaard, eds., *Material Culture and Other Things: Post-Disciplinary Studies in the 21st Century.* Gothenburg: Elanders Gotab, pp. 57–92.

Cornell, P., & Fahlander, F. (2007). Encounters-Materials-Confrontation: An Introduction. In P. Cornell & F. Fahlander eds., *Encounters-Materials-Confrontation. Archaeologies of Social Space and Interaction.* Cambridge: Cambridge Scholars Press, pp. 1–14.

Cruz, D. M. (2011). 'Pots Are Pots, Not People:' Material Culture and Ethnic Identity in the Banda Area (Ghana), Nineteenth and Twentieth Centuries. *Azania: Archaeological Research in Africa* **46**(3), 336–57.

Curta, F. (2014). Ethnic Identity and Archaeology. In C. Smith ed., *Encyclopedia of Global Archaeology.* Springer, New York, pp. 2507–14.

Darnell, J. C., & Manassa, C. (2007). *Tutankhamun's Armies: Battle and Conquest During Ancient Egypt's Late Eighteenth Dynasty.* New Jersey: John Wiley & Sons.

Davies, N. de Garis. (1922). *The Tomb of Puyemre at Thebes. Volume I: The Hall of Memories.* New York: The Metropolitan Museum of Arts.

Davies, N. de Garis. (1943). *The Tomb of Rekh-mir-rēē at Thebes.* Volume II. Publications of the Metropolitan Museum of Art Egyptian Expedition XI. New York: Metropolitan Museum of Art.

Derry, D. E. (1956). The Dynastic Race in Egypt. *The Journal of Egyptian Archaeology* **42**, 80–5.

Di Biase-Dyson, C. (2013). *Foreigners and Egyptians in the Late Egyptian Stories. Linguistic, Literary and Historical Perspectives.* Probleme der Ägyptologie 32. Leiden: Brill.

Eisenmann, S., et al. (2018). Reconciling Material Cultures in Archaeology with Genetic Data: The Nomenclature of Clusters Emerging from Archaeogenomic Analysis. *Nature. Scientific Reports* **2018**(8), 13003.

Emanuel, J. (2013). 'Šrdn from the Sea': The Arrival, Integration, and Acculturation of a 'Sea People'. *Journal of Ancient Egyptian Interconnections* **5**(1), 14–27.

Emery, W. B. (1965). *Egypt in Nubia*. London: Hutchinson of London.

Espinel, A. D. (2006). *Ethnicidad y territorio en el Egipto del Reino Antiguo*. Studia Aegyptiaca. Barcelona: Universitat Autònoma de Barcelona, Servei de Publicacions.

Feldman, M. H. (2006). *Diplomacy by Design. Luxury Arts and an 'International Style' in the Ancient Near East, 1400–1200 BCE*. Chicago: University of Chicago Press.

Fischer, M. M. J. (1986). Ethnicity and the Post-modern Arts of Memory. In J. Clifford & G. E. Marcus eds., *Writing Culture: The Poetics and Politics of Ethnography*. Berkeley: University of California Press, pp. 194–233.

Fischer-Bovet, Ch. (2018). Official Identity and Ethnicity: Comparing Ptolemaic and Early Roman Egypt. *Journal of Egyptian History* **11**(1–2), 208–42.

Forstner-Müller, I., & Müller, W. (2006). Die Entstehung des Hyksosstaates. Versuch einer sozioarchäologischen Modellbildung anhand der materiellen Kultur Tell el-Dab'as. In E. Czerny et al., ed., *Timelines. Studies in Honour of Manfred Bietak. Volume I*. Orientalia Lovaniensia Analecta 149. Leuven: Peeters, pp. 93–102.

Foster, H. J. (1974). The Ethnicity of the Ancient Egyptians. *Journal of Black Studies* **5**(2), 175–91.

Gliddon, G. R. (1843). *Ancient Egypt*. 10th ed. Revised and corrected. New York: W.M. Taylor & Co. Publishers.

Gordon, A. (2001). Foreigners. In D. B. Redford, ed., *The Oxford Encyclopaedia of Ancient Egypt*. Vol. 1. Oxford: Oxford University Press, pp. 544–8.

Goudriaan, K. (1988). *Ethnicity in Ptolemaic Egypt*. Dutch Monographs on Ancient History and Archaeology V. Amsterdam: J. C. Gieben.

Gould, S. J. (1996). *The Mismeasure of Man*. Revised and expanded. New York/ London: W.W. Norton & Company.

Gundacker, R. (2017). The Significance of Foreign Toponyms and Ethnonyms in Old Kingdom Text Sources. In F. Höflmayer, ed., *The Late Third Millennium in the Ancient Near East. Chronology, C14, and Climate Change*. The Oriental Institute of the University of Chicago Oriental Institute Seminars 11. Chicago: The University of Chicago, pp. 333–428.

Hall, T. (2014). Ethnicity and World-Systems Analysis. In J. McInerney, ed., *A Companion to Ethnicity in the Ancient Mediterranean*. Berkeley: Wiley-Blackwell, pp. 50–65.

Hallmann, S. (2006). *Die Tributszenen des Neuen Reiches*. Ägypten und Altes Testament 66. Wiesbaden: Harrassowitz.

Hakenbeck, S. E. (2019). Genetics, Archaeology and the Far Right: An Unholy Trinity. *World Archaeology* **51**, 517–27.

Haring, B. J. (2005). Occupation: Foreigner. Ethnic Difference and Integration in Pharaonic Egypt. In W. H. van Soldt, ed., *Ethnicity in Ancient Mesopotamia. Papers Read at the 48th Recontre Assyriologique Internationale, Leiden, 1–4 July 2002*. Leiden: Nederlands Instituut voor het Nabije Oosten, pp. 162–72.

Harvey, S. P. (1998). *The Cults of King Ahmose at Abydos*. Doctoral dissertation. University of Pennsylvania.

Hawkins, S. (2012). 'If Only I Could Accompany Him, This Excellent Marshman!': An Analysis of the Marshman (sXty) in Ancient Egyptian Literature. In C. Graves, G. Heffernan, L. McGarrity, E. Millward, & M. S. Bealby, eds., *Current Research in Egyptology 2012. Proceedings of the Thirteenth Annual Symposium University of Birmingham 2012*. Oxford: Oxbow Books, pp. 84–93.

Heath, J. (2005). *The Talking Greeks: Speech, Animals, and the Other in Homer, Aeschylus, and Plato*. Cambridge: Cambridge University Press.

Helck, W. (1977a). Fremde in Ägypten. In W. Helck & O. Eberhard, eds., *Lexikon der Ägyptologie II*, Wiesbaden: Harrassowitz, pp. 306–10.

Helck, W. (1977b). Fremdvölkerdarstellung. In W. Helck & O. Eberhard, eds., *Lexikon der Ägyptologie II*, Wiesbaden: Harrassowitz, pp. 316–21.

Hinson, B. (2014). Sinuhe's Life Abroad: Ethnoarchaeological and Philological Reconsiderations. In K. Accetta et al., eds., *Current Research in Egyptology 2013. Proceedings of the Fourteenth Annual Symposium. University of Cambridge, United Kingdom March 19 –22, 2013*. Oxford & Philadelphia: Oxbow Books, pp. 81–93.

Hodder, I. (1982). *Symbols in Action: Ethnoarchaeological studies of material culture*. Cambridge: Cambridge University Press.

Höflmayer, F. (2018). An Early Date for Khyan and Its Implications for Eastern Mediterranean Chronologies. In I. Forstner-Müller & N. Moeller, eds., *The Hyksos Ruler Khyan and the Early Second Intermediate Period in Egypt: Problems and Priorities of Current Research*. Proceedings of the Workshop of the Austrian Archaeological Institute and the Oriental Institute of the University of Chicago, Vienna, July 4 – 5, 2014. Wien: Holzhausen, 143–71.

Hu, D. (2013). Approaches to the Archaeology of Ethnogenesis: Past and Emergent Perspectives. *Journal of Archaeological Research* **21**, 371–402.

Hubschmann, C. (2010). Searching for the 'Archaeologically Invisible': Libyans in Dakhleh Oasis in the Third Intermediate Period. *Journal of the American Research Center in Egypt* **46**, 173–87.

Hutcheon, L., et al. (1998). Four Views on Ethnicity. *PMLA* **113**(1). Special Topic: Ethnicity, 28–51.

Isaac, B. (2004). *The Invention of Racism in Classical Antiquity*. Princeton and Oxford: Princeton University Press.

Jenkins, R. (2008). *Rethinking Ethnicity*. 2nd ed. Los Angeles: SAGE Publishing.

Johnson, J. H. (1999). Ethnic Considerations in Persian Period Egypt. In E. Teeter & J. A. Larson, eds., *Gold of Praise. Studies on Ancient Egypt in Honor of Edward F. Wente*. Studies in Ancient Oriental Civilization 58. Chicago: The Oriental Institute of the University of Chicago, pp. 211–22.

Jones, S. (1997). *The Archaeology of Ethnicity: Constructing Identities in the Past and Present*. London and New York: Routledge.

Kammerzell, F. (1993). *Studien zu Sprache und Geschichte der Karer in Ägypten*. Göttinger Oreintforschungen 27. Wiesbaden: Harrassowitz Verlag.

Keith, A. (1906). Were the Ancient Egyptians a Dual Race? *Man* **6**, 3–5.

Kemp, B. J. (2018). *Ancient Egypt: Anatomy of a Civilization*. 3rd ed. London and New York: Routledge.

Kilani, M. (2015). Between Geographical Imaginary and Geographical Reality: Byblos and the Limits of the World in the 18th Dynasty. In A. Belekdanian, Ch. Alvarez, S. Klein, & A-K. Gill, eds., *Current Research in Egyptology 2015. Proceedings of the Sixteenth Annual Symposium. University of Oxford 2015*. Oxford: Oxbow Books, pp.74–87.

Köhler, Ch. (2002). History or Ideology? New Reflections on the Narmer Palette and the Nature of Foreign Relations in Pre- and Early Dynastic Egypt. In E. C. M. van den Brink & Th. E. Levy, eds., *Egypt and the Levant. Interrelations from the 4th through the Early 3rd Millennium B.C.E.* London & New York: Leicester University Press, pp. 499–513.

Kristiansen, K. (2014). Towards a New Paradigm? The Third Science Revolution and its Possible Consequences in Archaeology. *Current Swedish Archaeology* **22**, 11–34.

Lakomy, K. (2016). *'Der Löwe auf dem Schlachtfeld' Das Grab KV 36 und die Bestattung des Maiherperi im Tal der Könige*. Wiesbaden: Reichert Verlag.

Lemos, R. (2020). Material Culture and Colonization in Ancient Nubia: Evidence from the New Kingdom Cemeteries. In C. Smith, ed., *Encyclopedia of Global Archaeology*. New York: Springer, pp. 1–25.

Lichtheim, M. (1976). *Ancient Egyptian Literature. Vol. II: New Kingdom*. Berkeley: UCLA Press.

Lilyquist, C. (2003). *The Tomb of Three Foreign Wives of Thutmose III*. New York: The Metropolitan Museum of Art.

Liszka, K. (2010). 'Medjay' (no. 188) in the Onomasticon of Amenemope. In Z. Hawass & J. H. Wegner, eds., *Millions of Jubilees Studies in Honor of David P. Silverman. Volume 1*. Le Caire: Conseil Suprême Des Antiquités De L'Égyptie, pp. 315–31.

Liszka, K. (2011). 'We Have Come from the Well of Ibhet': Ethnogenesis of the Medjay. *Journal of Egyptian History* **4**, 149–71.

Liszka, K. (2015). Are the Bearers of Pan-Grave Archaeological Culture Identical to Medjay-People in the Egyptian Textual Record? *Journal of Ancient Egyptian Interconnections* **7**(2), 42–60.

Liszka, K. (2017). Egyptian or Nubian? Dry-Stone Architecture at Wadi el-Hudi, Wadi es-Sebua, and the Eastern Desert. *The Journal of Egyptian Archaeology* **103**, 35–51.

Liszka, K. (2018). Discerning Ancient Identity: The Case of Aashyet's Sarcophagus (JE 47267). Journal of Egyptian History **11**, 185–207.

Loprieno, A. (1988). *Topos und Mimesis. Zum Ausländer in der ägyptischen Literatur.* Ägyptologische Abhandlungen 48. Wiesbaden: Otto Harrassowitz.

Lucy, S. (2005). Ethnic and Cultural Identities. In M. Díaz-Andreu, S. Lucy, S. Babić and D. N. Edwards, eds., *The Archaeology of Identity: Approaches to Gender, Age, Status, Ethnicity and Religion.* London and New York: Routledge, 86–109.

Maaranen, N., Zakrzewski, S., & Schutkowski, H. (2019). Hyksos in Egypt-utilising biodistance methods to interoret archaeological and textual evidence from Tell el-Dab^ca. *American Association of Physical Anthropologists Conference March 2019*, poster presentation.

Matić, U. (2014a). 'Nubian' Archers in Avaris: A Study of Culture-Historical Reasoning in Archaeology of Egypt. *Etnoantropološki problemi (Issues in Ethnology and Anthropology)* **9**(3), 697–721.

Matić, U. (2014b). 'Minoans', *kftjw* and the 'Islands in the Middle of wAD wr': Beyond Ethnicity. *Ägypten und Levante* **XXIV**, 277–94.

Matić, U. (2017). Der 'dritte Raum', Hybridität und das Niltal: Das epistemologische Potenzial der postkolonialen Theorie in der Ägyptologie. In S. Beck, B. Backes, & A. Verbovsek, eds., *Interkulturalität: Kontakt – Konflikt – Konzeptionalisierung, Beiträge des sechsten Berliner Arbeitskreis Junge Ägyptologie (BAJA 6) 13. 11.-15.11.2015.* Göttinger Orientforschung 63. Wiesbaden: Harrasowitz, pp. 93–112.

Matić, U. (2018a). De-colonizing Historiography and Archaeology of Ancient Egypt and Nubia Part 1: Scientific Racism. *Journal of Egyptian History* **11**(1–2), 19–44.

Matić, U. (2018b). 'Execration' of Nubians in Avaris: A case of mistaken ethnic identity and hidden archaeological theory. *Journal of Egyptian History* **11**(1–2), 87–112.

Matić, U. (2019). *Body and Frames of War in New Kingdom Egypt: Violent Treatment of Enemies and Prisoners.* Philippika 134. Wiesbaden: Harrassowitz.

Matić, U. (2020). *Violence and Gender in Ancient Egypt*. London and New York: Routledge.

McInerney, J. (2014). Ethnicity: An Introduction. In J. McInerney, ed., *A Companion to Ethnicity in the Ancient Mediterranean*. Berkeley: Wiley-Blackwell, pp. 1–16.

Meskell, L. (1999). *Archaeologies of Social Life: Age, Sex, Class Etcetera in Ancient Egypt*. Oxford: Blackwell.

Michaux-Colombot, D. (1994). The MDAY.W not Policemen but an Ethnic Group from the Eastern Desert. In C. Bonnet, ed., *Études Nubiennes. Conférence de Genève. Actes du VIIe Congres international d'études nubiennes 3–8 septembre 1990. Volume II. Communications*. Geneva: Société d'études nubiennes, pp. 29–36.

Michaux-Colombot, D. (2004). Geographical Enigmas related to Nubia. Medja, Punt, Meluhha and Magan. In T. Kendall, ed., *Nubian Studies 1998. Proceedings of the Ninth Conference of the International Society of Nubian Studies. August 21–26, 1998. Boston, Massachusetts*. Boston: Departement of African-American Studies, Northeastern University, pp. 353–63.

Michaux-Colombot, D. (2010). Identification of Meluhha Officers and Women with High Ranked Ramesside Medjay. In E. Kormysheva, ed., *Cultural Heritage of Egypt and Christian Orient. Proceedings of the Cairo Conference 29 Oct-3 Nov 2008, Institute of Oriental Studies RAS, Golenishev Egyptological Center*. Vol. 5. Moscow: Institute of Oriental Studies, Russian Academy of Sciences, pp. 165–90.

Michaux-Colombot, D. (2014). Pitfall Concepts in the Round of 'Nubia': Ta-sety, Nehesy, Medja, Maga and Punt Revisited. I J. R. Anderson & D. A. Welsby, eds., *The Fourth Cataract and Beyond: Proceedings of the 12th International Conference for Nubian Studies*. British Museum Publications on Egypt and Sudan 1. Leuven: Peeters, pp. 507–22.

Moers, G. (2001). *Fingierte Welten in der ägyptischen Literatur des 2. Jahrtausends v. Chr. Grenzüberschreitung, Reisemotiv und Fiktionalität*. Probleme der Ägyptologie 19. Leiden: Brill.

Moers, G. (2005). Auch der Feind war nur ein Mensch: Kursorisches zu einer Teilansicht pharaonischer Selbst- und Fremdwahrnehmungsoperationen. In H. Felber, ed., *Feinde und Aufrührer. Konzepte von Gegnerschaft in ägyptischen Texten besonders des Mittleren Reiches*. Abhandlungen der Sächsischen Akademie der Wissenschaften zu Leipzig 78,5. Stuttgart/Leipzig: Verlag der Sächsischen Akademie der Wissenschaften zu Leipzig, pp. 223–282.

Moers, G. (2016). 'Egyptian Identity'? Unlikely, and Never Rational. In H. Amstutz et al. eds., *Fuzzy Boundaries: Festschrift für Antonio Loprieno II*. Hamburg: Widmaier Verlag, pp. 693–704.

Moreno García, J. C. M. (2018). Ethnicity in Ancient Egypt: An Introduction to Key Issues. *Journal of Egyptian History* **11**(1–2), 1–17.

Morton, S. G. (1844). *Crania Aegyptiaca or Observations on Egyptian Ethnography derived from Anatomy, History and the Monuments*. London: Madden & Co.

Morris, E. (2018). *Ancient Egyptian Imperialism*. Hoboken: Wiley Blackwell

Mourad, A-L. (2015). *Rise of the Hyksos: Egypt and the Levant from the Middle Kingdom to the Early Second Intermediate Period*. Archaeopress Egyptology 11. Oxford: Archaeopress.

Mourad, A-L. (2017). Asiatic and Levantine(-Influenced) Products in Nubia: Evidence from the Middle Kingdom to the Early Second Intermediate Period. *Ägypten und Levante* **XXVII**, 381–401.

Niklasson, E. (2014). Shutting the Stable Door after the Horse has Bolted: Critical Thinking and the Third Science Revolution. *Current Swedish Archaeology* **22**, 57–63.

Normark, J. (2004). Discountinous Maya Identities-Culture and Ethnicity in Mayanist Discourse. In F. Fahlander & T. Oestigaard, eds., *Material Culture and Other Things: Post-Disciplinary Studies in the 21st Century*. Gothenburg: Elanders Gotab, pp. 109–60.

Nott, J. C., & Gliddon, G. R. (1854). *Types of Mankind or Ethnological Researches based upon the Ancient Monuments, Paintings, Sculptures, and Crania of Races*. London: Trübner & Co.

Obłuski, A. (2013). Dodekaschoinos in Late Antiquity. Ethnic Blemmyes vs. Political Blemmyes and the Arrival of Nobades. *Der Antike Sudan. Mitteilungen der Sudanarchäologischen Geselschaft zu Berlin e.V* 24: 141–7.

Olsen, R. (2013). The Medjay Leaders of the New Kingdom. In C. Graves et al., eds., *Current Research in Egyptology 2012. Proceedings of the Thirteenth Annual Symposium University of Birmingham 2012*. Oxford: Oxbow Books, pp. 145–56.

Pappa, E. (2013). Post-Colonial Baggage at the End of the Road: How to Put the Genie Back into Its Bottle and Where to Go from There. In W. P. van Pelt, ed., *Archaeology and Cultural Mixture*. Archaeological Review from Cambrdige 28.1. Cambridge: Archaeological Review from Cambridge, pp. 28–49.

Pemler, D. (2018). Looking at Nubians in Egypt: Nubian Women in New Kingdom Tomb and Temple Scenes and the Case of TT 40 (Amenemhet Huy). *Dotawo* **5**, 25–61.

Petrie, W. M. F. (1887). *Racial Photographs from the Egyptian Monuments*. London: R.C. Murray.

Petrie, W. M. F. (1901). The Races of Early Egypt. *The Journal of the Anthropological Institute of Great Britain and Ireland* **31**, 248–55.

Petrie, W. M. F., & Quibell, J. E. (1896). *Naqada and Ballas. 1895*. London: Bernard Quaritch.

Polz, D. (1998). Theben und Avaris: Zur 'Vertreibung' der Hyksos. In H. Guksch & D. Polz, Hrsgg, eds., *Stationen: Beiträge zur Kulturgeschichte Ägyptens. Rainer Stadelmann gewidmet*. Mainz: Philipp von Zabern, 219–31.

Quack, J. F. (1996). kft3w und i3śy. *Ägypten und Levante* **VI**, 75–81.

Quack, J. F. (2016). Von der schematischen Charakteristik bis zur ausgefeilten Ethnographie. Der Blick auf die Fremden durch die Alten Ägypter. *Zeitschrift der Deutschen Morgenländischen Gesellschaft* **166**(2), 289–316.

Raue, D. (2019a). Cultural Diversity of Nubia in the Later 3rd–Mid 2nd Millennium BC. In D. Raue, ed., *Handbook of Ancient Nubia*. Vol. I. Berlin: De Gruyter, pp. 293–334.

Raue, D. (2019b). Nubians in Egypt in the 3rd and 2nd Millennium BC. In D. Raue, ed., *Handbook of Ancient Nubia*. Vol. I. Berlin: De Gruyter, pp. 567–88.

Rebay-Salisbury, K. C. (2011). Thoughts in Circles: Kulturkreislehre as a Hidden Paradigm in Past and Present Archaeological Interpretations. In B. W. Roberts & M. V. Linden, eds., *Investigating Archaeological Cultures: Material Culture, Variability and Transmission*. New York: Springer, pp. 41–60.

Redford, D. (2004). *From Slave to Pharaoh: The Black Experience of Ancient Egypt*. Baltimore: Johns Hopkins University Press.

Redmount, C. A. (1995). Ethnicity, Pottery, and the Hyksos at Tell El-Maskhuta in the Egyptian Delta. *The Biblical Archaeologist* **58**(4), 182–90.

Rehak, P. (1998). Aegean Natives in Theban Tomb Paintings: The Keftiu Revisited. In E. H. Cline & D. H. Cline, eds., *The Aegean and the Orient in the Second Millennium*. Proceedings of the 50th Anniversary Symposium, Cincinnati, 18–20 April 1997. Aegaeum 18. Liège: Université de Liège, pp. 39–50.

Reisner, G. A. (1910). *The Archaeological Survey of Nubia: Report for 1907–1908 I. Archaeological Report*. Cairo: National Printing Department.

Reisner, G. A. (1923). *Excavations at Kerma I–III*. Harvard African Studies 5. Cambridge: Peabody Museum of Harvard University.

Retzmann, A. et al. (2019). The New Kingdom Population on Sai Island: Application of Sr Isotopes to Investigate Cultural Entanglement in Ancient Nubia. *Ägypten und Levante* **XXIX**, 355–80.

Riggs, C. (2005). *The Beautiful Burial in Roman Egypt: Art, Identity, and Funerary Religion*. Oxford: Oxford University Press.

Riggs, C., & Baines, J. (2012). Ethnicity. In E. Frood & W. Wendrich, eds., *UCLA Encyclopedia of Egyptology*, Los Angeles, pp. 1–16.

Rilly, C. (2019). Languages of Ancient Nubia. In D. Raue, ed., *Handbook of Ancient Nubia*. Vol. I. Berlin: De Gruyter, pp. 129–54.

Roberts, B. W., & Vander Linden, M. 2011. Investigating Archaeological Cultures: Material Culture, Variability, and Transmission. In B. W. Roberts & M. V. Linden, eds., *Investigating Archaeological Cultures. Material Culture, Variability and Transmission*. New York: Springer, pp. 1–22.

Roberts, R. G. (2013). Hyksos Self-Presentation and 'Culture'. In E. Frood & A. McDonald, eds., *Decorum and Experience: Essays in Ancient Culture for John Baines*. Oxford: Griffith Institute, pp. 285–90.

Roth, A. M. (1998). Ancient Egypt in America: Claiming the riches. In L. Meskell, ed., *Archaeology under Fire: Nationalism, Politics and Heritage in Eastern Mediterranean*. London & New York: Routledge, pp. 217–29.

Roth, A. M. (2015). Representing the Other: Non-Egyptians in Pharaonic Iconography. In M. K. Hartwig, ed., *A Companion to Ancient Egyptian Art*. Oxford: Wiley-Blackwell, 155–74.

Rowlandson, J. (2013). Dissing Thee Egyptians: Legal, Ethnic and Cultural Identities in Roman Egypt. In A. Gardner, E. Herring and K. Lomas, eds., *Creating Ethnicities & Identities in the Roman World*. London: Institute of Classical Studies, School of Advanced Study, University of London, pp. 213–47.

Safronov, A. (2017). Включало ли в себя египетское обозначение Сечет Эгеиду? [Did the Egyptian place-name St.t include designation of Aegean regions?] In N. N. Kazansky, ed., *Indo-European Linguistics and Classical Philology 21. Proceedings of the 21st Conference in Memory of Professor Joseph M. Tronsky. June 26–28, 2017.* St Petersburg: Nauka, pp. 748–57.

Said, E. (1978). *Orientalism*. New York: Pantheon Books.

Saini, A. (2019). *Superior: The Return of Race Science*. London: 4th Estate.

Saretta, Ph. (2016). *Asiatics in Middle Kingdom Egypt: Peceptions and Reality*. London: Bloomsbury.

Säve-Söderbergh, T. (1941). *Ägypten und Nubien, ein Beitrag zur Geschichte altägyptischer Aussenpolitik*. Lund: Håkan Ohlssons Boktryckeri.

Säve-Söderbergh, T., ed. (1987). *Temples and Tombs of Ancient Nubia: The International Rescue Campaign at Abu Simbel, Philae and Other Sites*. London: Thames & Hudson.

Schneider, T. (1998). *Ausländer in Ägypten während des Mittleren Reiches und der Hyksoszeit. Teil 1: Die ausländischen Könige*. Ägypten und Altes Testament. Studien zu Geschichte, Kultur und Religion Ägyptens und des Alten Testaments 42. Wiesbaden: Harrassowitz Verlag.

Schneider, T. (2003). Foreign Egypt: Egyptology and the Concept of Cultural Appropriation. *Ägypten und Levante* **XIII**, 155–161.

Schneider, T. (2010). Foreigners in Egypt: Archaeological Evidence and Cultural Context. In W. Wendrich, ed., *Egyptian Archaeology*. Oxford: Wiley-Blackwell, pp. 143–63.

Schneider, T. (2018). Ethnic Identities in Ancient Egypt and the Identity of Egyptology: Towards a 'Trans-Egyptology'. *Journal of Egyptian History* **11**(1–2), 243–6.

Schreg, R., et al. (2013). Habitus: ein soziologisches Konzept in der Archäologie. *Archäologische Informationen* **36**, 101–12.

Schuenemann, V. J., et al. (2017). Ancient Egyptian Mummy Genomes Suggest an increase of Sub-Saharan African ancestry in post-Roman periods. *Nature Communications* **8**.

Shaw, I. (2000). Egypt and the Outside World. In I. Shaw, ed., *Oxford History of Ancient Egypt*. Oxford: Oxford University Press, pp. 308–23.

Shaw, I., & Nicholson, P. (1995). *The British Museum Dictionary of Ancient Egypt*. Cairo: The American University in Cairo Press.

Sherratt, S. (2005). 'Ethnicities', 'ethnonyms' and archaeological labels. Whose ideologies and whose identities? In J. Clarke, ed., *Archaeological Perspectives on the Transmission and Transformation of Culture in the Eastern Mediterranean*. Oxford: Oxbow Books, pp. 25–38.

Siapkas, J. (2014). Ancient Ethnicity and Modern Identity. In J. McInerney, ed., *A Companion to Ethnicity in the Ancient Mediterranean*. Berkeley: Wiley-Blackwell, pp. 66–81.

Simpson, W. K. (1963). *Heka-nefer and the Dynastic Material from Toshka and Arminna*. Publications of the Pennsylvania-Yale Expedition to Egypt 1. New Haven: Peabody Museum.

Smith, S. T. (1991). A Model for Egyptian Imperialism in Nubia. *Göttinger Miszellen* **122**, 77–102.

Smith, S. T. (2003a). Pharaohs, Feasts and Foreigners: Cooking, Foodways and Agency on Ancient Egypt's Southern Frontier. In T. L. Bray, ed., *The Archaeology and Politics of Food and Feasting in Early States and Empires*. New York: Kluwer Academic Publishers, pp. 39–64.

Smith, S. T. (2003b). *Wretched Kush: Ethnic Identities and Boundaries in Egypt's Nubian Empire*. London & New York: Routledge.

Smith, S. T. (2007). Ethnicity and Culture. In T. Wilkinson, ed., *The Egyptian World*. London & New York: Routledge, pp. 218–41.

Smith, S. T. (2014). Nubian and Egyptian Ethnicity, In J. McInerney, ed., *A Companion to Ethnicity in the Ancient Mediterranean*. Berkeley: Wiley-Blackwell, pp. 194–212.

Smith, S. T. (2018). Ethnicity: Constructions of Self and Other in Ancient Egypt. *Journal of Egyptian History* **11**, 113–46.

Snape, S. (2003). The Emergence of Libya on the Horizon of Egypt. In D. O'Connor & S. Quirke, eds., *Mysterious Lands: Encounters with Ancient Egypt*. London: University College of London Press, pp. 93–106.

Sollors, W. (1989). *The Invention of Ethnicity*. New York: Oxford.

Sommer, U., & Gramsch, A. (2011). German Archaeology in Context: An Introduction to History and Present of Central European Archaeology. In U. Sommer & A. Gramsch, eds., *A History of Central European Archaeology. Theory, Method, and Politics*. Budapest: Archaeolingua, pp. 7–39.

de Souza, A. (2013). The Egyptianisation of the Pan-Grave Culture: A New Look at an Old Idea. *The Bulletin of the Australian Centre for Egyptology* **24**, 109–26.

de Souza, A. (2019). *New Horizons: The Pan-Grave ceramic tradition in context*. Middle Kingdom Studies 9. London: Golden House Publications.

Sparks, R. (2004). Canaan in Egypt: Archaeological Evidence for a Social Phenomenon. In J. Bourriau & J. Phillips, eds., *Invention and Innovation: The Social Context of Technological Change 2, Egypt, the Aegean and the Near East, 1650–1150*. Oxford: Oxbow Books, pp. 27–56.

Spencer, N., Stevens, A., & Binder, M. (2017). Introduction: History and Historiography of a Colonial Entanglement, and the Shaping of New Archaeologies for Nubia in the New Kingdom. In N. Spencer, A. Stevens, & M. Binder, eds., *Nubia in the New Kingdom: Lived Experience, Pharaonic Control and Indigenous Traditions*. British Museum Publications on Egypt & Sudan 3. Leuven: Peeters, pp. 1–64.

Spivak, G. Ch. (1988). Can the Subaltern Speak? In C. Nelson & G. Lawrence, ed., *Marxism and the Interpretation of Culture*. Urbana: University of Illinois Press, pp. 271–313.

Stantis, Ch. et al. (2020). Who Were the Hyksos? Challenging Traditional Narratives Using Strontium Isotope ($87Sr/86Sr$) Analysis of Human Remains from Ancient Egypt. *Plos One* 15(7): e0235414. https://doi.org/10.1371/journal.pone.0235414

Steel, L. (2018). Shifting Relations in Bronze Age Gaza: An Investigation into Egyptianizing Practices and Cultural Hybridity in the Southern Levant during the Late Bronze Age. *Journal of Ancient Egyptian Interconnections* **20**, 15–30.

Stockhammer, P. W. (2012). Entangled Pottery: Phenomena of Appropriation in the Late Bronze Age Eastern Mediterranean. In J. Maran & P. W. Stockhammer, eds,. *Materiality and Social Practice. Transformative Capacities of Intercultural Encounters*. Oxford: Oxbow, pp. 89–103.

Stockhammer, P. W. (2013). From Hybridity to Entanglement, From Essentialism to Practice. In W. P. van Pelt, ed., *Archaeology and Cultural Mixture*. Archaeological Review from Cambridge 28.1. Cambridge: Archaeological Review from Cambridge, pp. 11–28.

Thomas, J. (2004). *Archaeology and Modernity*. London & New York: Routledge.

Trigger, B. G. (1976). *Nubia under the Pharaohs*. London: Thames & Hudson.

Trigger, B. G. (2008). *A History of Archaeological Thought*. 2nd ed. Cambridge: Cambridge University Press.

Van Pelt, W. P. (2013). Revising Egypto-Nubian Relations in New Kingdom Lower Nubia: From Egyptianization to Cultural Entanglement. *Cambridge Archaeological Journal* **23**(3), 523–550.

Van Valkenburgh, P. (2013). Hybridity, Creolization, Mestizaje: A Comment. In W. P. van Pelt, ed., *Archaeology and Cultural Mixing*. Archaeological Review from Cambridge 28.1. Cambridge: Archaeological Review from Cambridge, pp. 301–22.

Verbovsek, A., Backes, B., & Jones, C. eds. (2011) *Methodik und Didaktik in der Ägyptologie: Herausforderungen eines kulturwissenschaftlichen Paradigmenwechsels in den Altertumswissenschaften*. Ägyptologie und Kulturwissenschaft 4. München: Wilhelm Fink Verlag.

Vittmann, G. (2003). *Ägypten und die Fremden im ersten vorchristlichen Jahrtausend*. Mainz am Rhein: Verlag Philipp von Zabern.

Voss, B. L. (2008). *The Archaeology of Ethnogenesis. Race and Sexuality in Colonial San Francisco*. Berkeley: University of California Press.

Walsh, C. (2018). Kerma Ceramics, Commensality Practices, and Sensory Experiences in Egypt during the Late Middle Bronze Age. *Journal of Ancient Egyptian Interconnections* **20**, 31–51.

Weiner, S. (2010). *Microarchaeology: Beyond the Visible Archaeological Record*. Cambridge: Cambridge University Press.

Wendrich, W., ed. (2010). *Egyptian Archaeology*. Oxford: Wiley-Blackwell.

Williams, F. E., Belcher, R. L., & Armelagos, G. J. (2005). Forensic Misclassification of Ancient Nubian Crania: Implications for Assumptions about Human Variation. *Current Anthropology* **46**(2), 340–6.

Wilson, J. A. (1969). Egyptian Hymns and Prayers. In J. B. Pritchard, ed., *Ancient Near Eastern Texts Relating to the Old Testament*. Princeton: Princeton University Press, pp. 365–81.

Winnicki, J. K. (1992). Demotische Stelen aus Terenuthis. In J. Johnson, ed., *Life in a Multi-Cultural Society: Egypt from Cambyses to Constantine and Beyond*. Studies in Ancient Oriental Civilization 51. Chicago: The University of Chicago Press, pp. 351–60.

de Wit, T. (2015). Enemies of the State;: Preceptions of 'Otherness' and State Formation in Egypt. In P. Kousoulis & N. Lazaridis, eds., *Proceedings of the Tenth International Congress of Egyptologists, University of the Aegean, Rhodes, 22–29 May 2008*. Orientalia Lovaniensia Analecta 241. Leuven: Peeters, 649–67.

Woodward, J., et al. (2015). Shifting Sediment Sources in the World's Longest River: A Strontium Isotope Record for the Holocene Nile. *Quarternary Science Reviews* **130**, 124–40.

Zakrzewski, S., Shortland, A., & Rowland, J. (2016). *Science in the Study of Ancient Egypt*. London & New York: Routledge.

Zibelius-Chen, K. (2007). Die Medja in altägyptischen Quellen. *Studien zur Altägyptischen Kultur* **36**, 391–405.

Acknowledgements

I am grateful to all of the people who discussed this topic with me over the past years and as there are many I can only do justice by expressing my gratitude to the few of them with whom I had most intensive discussions: Angelika Lohwasser, Irene Forstner-Müller, Wolfgang Müller, Constance von Rüden, Dietrich Raue, Bettina Bader, and Christian Knoblauch. I also thank Andrea Sinclair for proofreading the English of my manuscript and encouraging this debate, and Astrid Hassler for her help with the graphics.

I would like to thank Juan Carlos Moreno García, Gianluca Miniaci, and Anna Stevens for inviting me to contribute to the series Elements: Ancient Egypt in Context with this text and for being patient with my slight delay. I am also grateful to two anonymous reviewers who provided useful comments which helped in producing a more focused and readable text.

I dedicate this text to my brother Nikola Matić.

Cambridge Elements ≡

Ancient Egypt in Context

Gianluca Miniaci
University of Pisa
Gianluca Miniaci is Associate Professor in Egyptology at the University of Pisa, Honorary Researcher at the Institute of Archaeology, UCL–London, and Chercheur associé at the École Pratique des Hautes Études, Paris. He is currently co-director of the archaeological mission at Zawyet Sultan (Menya, Egypt). His main research interest focuses on the social history and the dynamics of material culture in the Middle Bronze Age Egypt and its interconnections between the Levant, Aegean, and Nubia.

Juan Carlos Moreno García
CNRS, Paris
Juan Carlos Moreno García (PhD in Egyptology, 1995) is a CNRS senior researcher at the University of Paris IV-Sorbonne, as well as lecturer on social and economic history of ancient Egypt at the École des Hautes Études en Sciences Sociales (EHESS) in Paris. He has published extensively on the administration, socio-economic history, and landscape organization of ancient Egypt, usually in a comparative perspective with other civilizations of the ancient world, and has organized several conferences on these topics.

Anna Stevens
University of Cambridge and Monash University
Anna Stevens is a research archaeologist with a particular interest in how material culture and urban space can shed light on the lives of the non-elite in ancient Egypt. She is Senior Research Associate at the McDonald Institute for Archaeological Research and Assistant Director of the Amarna Project (both University of Cambridge).

About the Series
The aim of this Elements series is to offer authoritative but accessible overviews of foundational and emerging topics in the study of ancient Egypt, along with comparative analyses, translated into a language comprehensible to non-specialists. Its authors will take a step back and connect ancient Egypt to the world around, bringing ancient Egypt to the attention of the broader humanities community and leading Egyptology in new directions.

Cambridge Elements ≡

Ancient Egypt in Context

Elements in the Series

CPSIA information can be obtained
at www.ICGtesting.com
Printed in the USA
LVHW021647180421
684847LV00006B/140